D0457253

Look What Love Has Done

Look What Love Has Done

Five-Minute Messages to Lift Your Spirit

JOSEPH WALKER

SHADOW
MOUNTAIN

Visit us at shadowmountain.com

Library of Congress Cataloging-in-Publication Data

Walker, Joseph, 1955-
   Look what love has done : five-minute messages to lift your spirit /Joseph Walker.
        p. cm.
     ISBN-13 978-1-59038-710-8 (hardbound : alk. paper)
     ISBN-10 1-59038-710-4 (hardbound : alk. paper)
     1. Life. 2. Encouragement. I. Title.
BD450.W235 2007
242—dc22   2006032143

Printed in the United States of America
Edwards Brothers, Incorporated, Lillington, NC

10   9   8   7   6   5   4   3   2   1

Contents

Acknowledgments

This book is lovingly dedicated to all whose stories are contained herein. Thank you for sharing your thoughts, your experiences, and your lives with me—and for allowing me to share them with others. My greatest and most profound wish is that these messages, however brief, may provide some measure of insight, encouragement, inspiration, and hope to those who read them. Certainly they have provided that for me, and I thank you all for the significant part you have played in helping make this book a reality.

I also extend heartfelt thanks to:

Kathleen Lubeck, whose vision and guidance resulted in the creation of ValueSpeak, the weekly newspaper column from which most of these stories are drawn;

Numerous newspaper editors and online e-zine publishers who understand what I'm trying to say and who bravely and loyally buck the trend of contemporary media negativism;

Mrs. Stallings, my fifth-grade teacher, who sparked a flame in me when she laughed out loud at my first feeble attempt at literary creativity (who would have thought that a joking reference to "J. Paul Getty's private resort, the Spa Getty," would lead to this?);

Cory Maxwell, Chris Schoebinger, and Richard Peterson, of Shadow Mountain, who have magically—and skillfully—transformed a newspaper guy into a book guy;

And faithful readers, who . . . well, what is more important to a writer than people who are willing to read what he writes?

Mostly, however, I'm thankful to thirteen extraordinary people who fill my heart with love and who imbue my life with meaning: Anita, AmyJo, Brock, Samantha, Joe Jr., Jen, Becky, Julieanne, Emily, Andrea, Adam, Elizabeth, and Jon. You'll see those names fairly frequently on these pages. There's a good reason for that:

I write about life, and they ARE my life. My wife, my children (and their spouses), and my grandchildren are for me the literal embodiment of this book's declarative title: "Look what love has done!"

To all of you, and to my parents, my brothers and sisters, nieces and nephews, neighbors and friends, I express my thanks and gratefully acknowledge your impact on my words and my life.

Look What Love Has Done!

Spring is a time of renewal. A time to start over. A time to begin again.

And, yes, I know how illogical that last expression is. Speaking grammatically, one can begin a thing and then one can do it again. But one cannot "begin again," since one can only begin a thing once.

At least, that's what I used to think.

And then I met Mark.

Mark had experienced more pain and greater challenges in his six years of living than most of us encounter in a lifetime. His mother began abusing him even before he was born by taking into her body substances that damaged his developing body. The abuse continued after his birth in a variety of ways too despicable to mention.

As a result, Mark's sixth birthday was hardly a cause

for celebration. He was about the size of a 3-year-old and functioned physically and mentally on a level even younger than that. He couldn't walk. He couldn't speak. He couldn't even breathe without the help of a tube inserted in his throat. He was partially deaf, partially blind, and no one was sure how much he could understand of what was going on around him. He never smiled, which is understandable because the only happy thing in his life was the fact that he had been abandoned by his abusive mother.

Pathetic? Perhaps. But hopeless? No way.

On the other side of the country from where Mark was born, a single mother was longing for a second child. Unfortunately, the only man in her life was her 9-year-old son, Damien, and most conventional adoption agencies wouldn't even consider Donna as an adoptive parent.

So she started trying to work out something unconventional. She contacted agencies that specialize in hard-to-place children and found them to be much more open to her desire to adopt. Eventually she heard about Mark. She started loving him almost immediately.

"It'll be hard," a social worker warned her.

"That's okay," Donna said. "I'm tough."

"But he's got all of these medical problems."

"That's okay," Donna said. "I'm a nurse."

"But he's black and you're white."

"That's okay," Donna said. "I'm color blind."

So Donna flew across the country to pick up her new son and bring him home to nurse, nurture, and love. They returned, appropriately enough, on Valentine's Day, and Mark began progressing immediately—and remarkably. Within a short period of time he was walking and learning to do things for himself. It turned out he could see and hear better than anyone thought he could, and he was able to understand quite a bit. And within a few months they took that tube out of his throat so he could breathe normally for the first time in his life.

Oh, and there's one other thing he started doing: smiling. A lot. Especially when he was snuggled on his new mother's shoulder.

"People are amazed at how well Mark is doing," Donna told me. "They call it a miracle. And maybe it is. But it isn't a surprise. Everyone knows that love is a power. It's just that Mark has never really experienced it—until now."

Donna smiled as Mark toddled into his big brother's arms, smiling every step of the way.

"And now," she said, "just look at what love has done!"

Love gave Mark a new life. It gave him a home. And more than anything else, it truly gave him a chance to begin again.

Which, come to think of it, is just as it should be in the spring.

Memorial Day Memories

It is Memorial Day, 2051.

Rebecca, a handsome middle-aged woman, stands with her children in a small community cemetery in the valley where she was born. It has been years since she has been here, and she can't help but wonder why. Every time she comes back, she wonders why she doesn't come more often. Sometimes she wonders why she ever left.

Spring is beautiful here—surpassingly so. From the green-covered mountains rising majestically on every side, to the lake bulging with spring runoff, stretching to cover the valley floor. Just being here speaks peace to her heart and comfort to Rebecca's soul—a rare and precious thing during times teeming with callous uncertainty.

Which is part of what brought her here—a search for peace. But only part. She recently learned that she is about to become a grandmother—a thrilling, daunting prospect if ever there was one. As a result, she has found herself thinking a lot about her grandparents and what they meant in her life. She was drawn here, as if walking among their headstones would somehow transfer their accumulated knowledge and experience to her.

Of course, finding the graves in the cemetery will be the first challenging part of her search. After all, it has been years . . .

"Here they are!" Her 16-year-old son, a tall, blond, handsome young man, proclaims his discovery. In no time the family is gathered at the two headstones, reading them as if the information on them was new and interesting.

"This is my Grandpa Joseph Walker and my Grammy Anita," Rebecca announces. "I was their first grandchild, and they spoiled me constantly. I wish you could have known them."

She tells her family about her tender, loving Grammy Anita. About all of the times they played together, and talked together, and shopped together, and laughed together.

"You could just feel her love in everything she said and did," she says, almost reverently. "She was about the best grandma a little girl could have."

She pauses for a moment, lost in the crisp, clear memory of childhood outings and overnighters, her eyes moist and red. Then she wipes a tear from her cheek and shifts her focus.

"Then there was Grandpa Joe," she says, smiling. "What a character. He . . . he . . ."

He what?

That's the question I'm pondering this Memorial Day. What are the memories my granddaughter, Rebecca, and my other grandchildren will have of me, fifty or so Memorial Days from now? Right now, she thinks I'm terrific—not as terrific as Grammy Anita, but terrific nonetheless. When she sees me she runs to me, holding out her chubby little arms, calling out "Bampa! Bampa!"

Okay, okay—so maybe I'm bribing her with chocolate. All's fair in love and grandparenting.

The point is, I'm making the memories now that will be remembered at my graveside many Memorial Days from now. So are you. It's a simple fact of life, one I become more aware of as I grow older. And I can't help but wonder, what sort of memories will they be? Will they be pleasant? Happy? Joyful? Or will they be wistful and sad? It's up to us—right now. Today.

Because by Memorial Day 2051, it will be too late.

The Treasure in the Box

Did you see the news story about the teacher who found an old cigar box in her attic? When she opened it she saw that it was full of old papers. She was about to toss it into the trash when she noticed the word *stock* on one of the papers. Upon further inspection she discovered that the box was filled with old stock certificates. Just for fun she had their value assessed.

You guessed it: instant millionaire.

"I don't imagine my life will be all that much different," she said after banking her newfound fortune. "I may buy some new shoes. Other than that, I won't be making many changes."

Personally, I think wealth is wasted on such people. What's the point of being suddenly prosperous if you're not going to allow yourself to suddenly . . . you know . . . prosper?

I know I would. I know this because I've been thinking about it all week—or at least since my dad's wife, Jean, called to tell me about a box she found while spring cleaning.

"There are some real treasures in these boxes," she said. "You ought to have them."

"Treasures?" I asked. "What sort of treasures?"

"Oh, you know—jewelry, certificates, a little money, and there are some metals that are absolutely precious."

Jewelry? Certificates? Money? Precious metals? And she wants to give them to me?

Ka-ching!

Unlike the teacher in the news story, I could come up with plenty of ideas for improving my life once those treasures made their way into my bank account. Most involved quitting my job and buying a Winnebago. By the time I got the box from Jean, I had already imagined myself back and forth across the country and all the way to Hawaii (with and without the Winnebago, respectively).

In the privacy of my car, I carefully opened the black jewelry box. Inside, it was just as she had promised: jewelry, certificates, money and precious metals. Only the jewelry was costume jewelry in brilliant blues, reds and aquamarines. The certificates included my mother's high school diploma. The money was an English penny. And the precious "metals" were actually precious medals, including one awarded to my great-grandfather for being an "Indian War Veteran" and another presented to my great-great-grandfather for helping to pioneer the American West.

Okay, I'll admit it: I was disappointed at first. There was nothing of any value here—unless you counted sentimental value. But the more I studied the stuff in the box, the more like a treasure it seemed to be. And the more like a mystery. What did my great-grandmother's garish red rhinestone broach tell me about the personality of a woman I never met? Am I the only one in the family who will be surprised to learn that Mom graduated from high school in Denver? Who wore the dangly blue pendant and why did it smell—vaguely but distinctively—of turpentine? And what about the cool reading spectacles? What was the deal with those?

I'm not exactly sure where to look for the answers to these questions. But we're going to have a lot of fun trying to find them. Meanwhile, I'm enjoying this wonderful sense of connection as I handle and admire objects that were obviously cherished by my ancestors. It makes me feel grounded. It makes me feel like I belong. It makes me feel like I'm part of something that extends beyond the here and now. And that feeling is something I value and treasure.

Regardless of the value of the treasure in the box.

Someone to Take the Blame

I thought it would be a great April Fools' Day prank. Honest—that's what I was thinking.

I mean, it was a glorious spring day. We were growing teenagers. We needed to spend 45 minutes out in the fresh air, frolicking in the sun while the fire department cleared the school. From my eighteen-year-old perspective, it would be healthy. Fun. Exhilarating. Liberating.

But Principal Perkins didn't see it that way.

"I want to know who set off the fire alarm, and I want to know NOW!" I heard him growl at Mr. Mangus, his assistant principal, as we started filing back into the high school. "Whoever did this is going to be in SERIOUS trouble!"

I wanted to ask him exactly how serious SERIOUS

trouble would be, but I didn't dare. I was a senior, just a little more than a month away from graduation. College scholarships were at stake, and Vietnam beckoned to those who didn't qualify—especially if you had a high draft number like I did. I didn't need SERIOUS trouble.

Besides—and this is a little embarrassing to admit, given the circumstances—I was the student body president. Principal Perkins trusted me. A couple of months earlier he had allowed some of my friends and I to stay overnight in the school to "protect" it from pranksters the night before our Big Game against our cross-town rivals. He even provided the pizza, for Pete's sake! How could I face him now—guilty of prankster-ism in the first degree?

I tried to look inconspicuous as Mr. Mangus roamed the halls, asking questions. What if they dusted for fingerprints? My fingerprints were all over the school. It wouldn't be hard to match them to mine. Then . . . hello, Hanoi Hilton.

I was opening my locker, wondering if it would help to crawl inside and close the door behind me, when I heard a voice behind me.

"I saw what you did."

I froze. I was busted. I turned slowly to face my accuser. Thankfully, it wasn't Mr. Mangus. It was John, a 19-or-20-year-old senior (Okay, so he had a little trouble with 5th grade—twice) who spent more time in the parking lot than the classroom. And he was smiling.

"Nice job, man!" he said, punching me playfully in the shoulder. "That was great! And nobody will ever guess it was you! It was, like, the perfect crime!"

"Not quite perfect if you saw me," I whispered. "John, did anyone else see . . . ?"

"Mr. Walker!"

It was Mr. Mangus storming toward me, and he wasn't smiling. John retreated to the other side of the hall, and I braced myself to be unceremoniously stripped of title, rank, and privilege—you know, like on the opening of that TV show, *Branded*.

"Mr. Walker, I've talked to several students who say they saw you near where the fire alarm was pulled this morning," Mr. Mangus said sharply. "Did you see anything?"

"Well, no," I said, choosing my words carefully. "I mean . . . you know . . . I saw . . . um . . . regular stuff . . . but not . . . you know . . . anyone close to the alarm . . . specifically . . ."

Mr. Mangus had spent a lifetime dealing with high school students. He knew an intentionally vague answer when he heard one. And it immediately made him suspicious. "So if you didn't SEE anyone," he said, "perhaps you were . . . somehow . . . involved . . . ?"

There it was. A direct question. If I answered honestly, I was in SERIOUS trouble. If I lied and it was later discovered that I lied, well, Watergate would look like an April Fools' Day prank by comparison. But before I could respond I heard that voice behind me. Again.

"Bennie, you're amazing."

Mr. Mangus didn't take kindly to students calling him by his first name. He whirled to face John. "How many times do I have to tell you not to call me—"

"Do you really think Walker here would do something like that?"

"Well, I don't know, John. I wouldn't have thought so, but . . ."

"Gimme a break," John said. "He's a ['goody-goody']."

I didn't know whether to be relieved or insulted.

"Well, then who did it, John?" Mr. Mangus asked. Then he pressed: "Was it you?"

John didn't hesitate. "Yeah, it was me," he said. "What are you gonna do about it?"

"It isn't what I'm going to do," Mr. Mangus said as he took John firmly by the arm and started leading him down the hall. "It's what Principal Perkins is going to do. I'm just going to watch. And I'm going to enjoy every minute of it."

I wish I could tell you that I jumped to John's defense and admitted my guilt. I didn't. He was willing—even anxious—to take the blame for me. And I was willing to let him—guilty though I was. I never did find out what SERIOUS trouble John got into, but it turns out he had already enlisted in the Marines. I heard he won some medals for bravery and courage, and it didn't surprise me in the least.

I think about John every year about this time—not because of April Fools', but rather because of Easter.

Because there are other things of which I've been guilty.

And because Someone was willing to take the blame for me.

Matricide at the Rustic Rink

To this day I can't tell you why that Cub Scout roller skating party was so all-fired important to me. For some reason, I was absolutely obsessed with going to the Rustic Rink with all my fellow Cubs and lacing on a pair of heavy black roller skates.

But there was a problem. It was a Cubs-and-Parents affair, which meant that I had to invite Mom and Dad. Which was okay, except for one thing. I had long since figured out that my parents were a little different from most of my friends' folks. For one thing, they were older—Dad was 53 at the time, Mom was 47—and both were physically less active than other parents in the neighborhood. My friends would go skiing and camping with their parents. Mine let me watch *The Mickey Mouse Club* nearly every day.

Which is why it surprised me a little when Mom responded so positively to the skating party when I finally found the courage to bring it up.

"But I've never been roller skating before," Dad protested.

"Then it's time you learned," Mom replied. "Besides, you used to ice skate."

"Wanda, that was forty years ago."

"Oh, you know how it is with those kinds of things," Mom assured him. "Once you learn them you never forget them." She placed her hands lovingly on my shoulders. "If it means so much to him, Bud, don't you think we should at least give it a try?"

Dad looked at me with mock frustration.

"All right," he said with a shrug and a chuckle. Then he pointed a finger directly at me. "But you better plan on following right behind me so I can land on you when I fall."

Actually, that job fell to Mom. Since she had actually roller skated when she was young, she was designated as the couple's Skating Expert. It was her task to support Dad as he made his herky-jerky, clackety-clacking way around the rink and to go down with him whenever he fell, which was about once every twenty yards. The two of them would sit on the floor after each fall, giggling like teenagers, and then they would struggle to their feet and begin again.

Clackety-clack. Thud. Ha-ha-ha.

Only I wasn't laughing. Most of the other parents skated pretty well. Ron and Don's dad could skate backwards, for Pete's sake. But there was my roly-poly Mom trying to support my nearly white-haired father, who couldn't seem to grasp the concept of gliding on skates. They went down—again and again—in an embarrassing gale of laughter, making enough noise that you could barely hear the Beach Boys tunes blaring from the rink's loudspeakers.

I don't think I even told my parents "thank you" as we drove home from the party that night. I vaguely remember hearing my Mom mention that her back was a little sore, but mostly I was up to my earlobes in humiliation and self-pity.

My mortification turned to shame when Mom awakened in the middle of the night, her back in agony. Dad gave her aspirin. He alternated putting a heating pad on her back and then massaging it until dawn. Though she tried to be brave, Mom couldn't keep from moaning in pain—low and guttural—and tears rolled down her cheeks until her pillow glistened with moisture. I tried to sleep through it, but it was impossible with the remorse that enveloped me. As the first light of day peeked over the mountains, Dad prepared to take Mom to the emergency room. I heard him sadly tell my sister that it was his fault for being so darn clumsy.

But I knew whose fault it really was. When I finally saw her in the hospital, I was almost overwhelmed with guilt. She had slipped a disc in her back and was in traction, which looked to me like something straight out of a torture chamber. Her head was held in place by an ugly assortment of cables and harnesses that kept her looking straight ahead. A stack of weights was attached to her feet, seeming to turn her into the rope in a painful game of tug-of-war.

And I had put her there. For all I knew, I could have

killed her. For the first time I understood how selfless her concern for me had been. And how selfish I had been.

"Mom . . ." I could barely speak.

"Joey? Is that you, Son? I'm sorry, I can't see you." Again she was apologizing for something that wasn't her fault. I figured it was my turn to ask forgiveness.

"Mom . . . last night . . . the roller skating . . ." I couldn't even form the words.

"Oh, yes—the roller skating," she said. Then she smiled as best she could in that harness. "We did have a wonderful time, didn't we?"

In time Mom recovered from the injuries she suffered at the Rustic Rink. Thankfully, I hadn't killed her. But her back was never the same.

And neither, I hope, was I.

Car Pool 500

I did it for Beth. Honest—I did.

We were running a little late, and I didn't want her to get a blemish on her attendance record. So when I noticed that long line of cars backing up next to the cemetery waiting to merge onto the main road in front of us, I became . . . , you know . . . anxious.

"Come on . . ." I said . . . you know . . . anxiously to the drivers ahead of me, "get out there! Be bold! Be aggressive! Take a chance!"

"Uh, Dad," Beth said, "I don't think they can hear you."

Beth is just sixteen and is a fairly new and inexperienced driver. She still thinks I'm just talking to myself when I give instructions to all the drivers around me. Eventually she'll learn how important this is to maintaining equilibrium on the roadway and balance in the universe.

But on this morning it wasn't working. The line wasn't moving. And the clock was ticking on Beth's attendance record.

So I decided to take my own advice. Boldly I veered off the main road and onto a service road through the cemetery. I sped aggressively through the cemetery and took a chance darting out onto the main road on the other side. My maneuver was so impressively successful that when I glanced in the rear-view mirror I noticed someone in a light blue pickup following my lead.

Suddenly, for the first time in my life, I understood NASCAR. The speed. The strategy. The adrenaline. The left turns.

Flushed with success, I turned to Beth, who had the same expression on her face that she had after she saw that movie about the baby-sitter who had to deal with a crazed man in her house. A new strategy seemed in order.

"Uh, you don't need to mention that little detour to your mother," I said.

"Don't worry," she said as she worked to extricate her fingernails from the armrest. "Mom already knows you drive like a maniac."

I smiled. Among NASCAR drivers this is considered a compliment.

My drive home was sort of like a victory lap. I could almost imagine my pit crew drizzling milk all over me as I posed for pictures with the queen of the Car Pool 500.

"I did it all for Beth!" I would shout as cameras flashed all around me.

I was still feeling pretty euphoric when I approached the cemetery on my way back and noticed red and blue flashing lights on the service road. As I got closer I could see two police cars surrounding a light blue pickup—the same light blue pickup that had followed me onto the service road just a few minutes earlier. The young driver—he looked to be about Beth's age—was sitting on a bench, his baseball-capped head in his hands, as the officers prepared the citation that was probably going to complicate the young man's life considerably.

I'm embarrassed to admit that my first thought was: Whew! I had dodged a bullet—or at least, a traffic ticket.

Then the guilt hit. I found myself wondering about the part I had played in the little police drama unfolding on the cemetery service road. Did the boy take that route because he had seen me do it? Would he have even thought of it had I not blazed such a glorious trail before him? And what had I taught my daughter about safe, sane, responsible driving?

One of the most meaningful things one generation can leave to the next is the power of example. Obviously, I had failed in this significant responsibility the morning of the Car Pool 500—NASCAR points notwithstanding. But I hereby resolve to do better.

And to do it for Beth.

When "No" Is Actually "Yes"

Mom wasn't a great typist, but she was better at it than I was. She had to be. She was a receptionist/assistant/mother hen for a local obstetrician. Typing was just one of the many services she offered, along with scheduling appointments, rejoicing with those who had reason to rejoice (and comforting those who did not), and taping cartoons (most of them lampooning doctors) on the ceiling above the examining table so patients had something to occupy their minds while the doctor was ... you know ... doctoring.

I, on the other hand, was a high school sophomore who typed like a mother hen searching for grub worms: hunt and peck. Hunt and peck. Hunt and ... oops!

Where's the White-out?

So I assumed Mom would see the wisdom of my plan as clearly as I could.

"You want me to WHAT?" she asked when I mentioned it one evening after dinner.

"Type up my debate cards," I said, only a tad less confidently than I said it the first time.

"So you're basically asking me to do your homework for you?"

"No—not at all," I assured her. "I'll do all the research. I'll find the quotes and I'll organize them. I just need you to . . . you know . . . type them."

The more I said it the better I liked it.

"And how many of these cards will there be?" she wanted to know.

"Oh, just a few dozen this year," I said. "But Mr. B says that if we do well and make the debate team next year we'll be typing hundreds and hundreds of cards." I hesitated then added: "Won't that be great? Think of all the time we'll get to spend together!"

Mom smiled. "It sounds like you need to learn to type," she said. "And these debate cards are going to provide you with a wonderful opportunity to learn!"

Which is when Mom introduced me to the Green Monster, an avocado-colored typewriter that was just a step above pounding out letters with a hammer and chisel. A very small step.

The Green Monster was a portable typewriter, as long as your definition of the word *portable* includes "something that can only be moved from place to place by two linebackers and an intricate system of winches and pulleys." And it was a manual typewriter, which meant you had to push each letter key hard enough that this long arm would come out and strike the paper through black tape. The only thing missing was a little prehistoric bird perched on the end to squawk "Ding!" when you reached the end of a row—otherwise it was positively Flintstonian.

To be honest, I was pretty hurt that Mom wouldn't type my debate cards for me. Other moms were doing it for their kids. Why wouldn't my mother do this one small thing for me?

"You can do this," Mom would calmly say every time I whined about how hard it was to push the keys on the

Green Monster. "Before long you'll be the fastest typist in the class."

That didn't happen. But by the time I got to college I was pretty darn fast, especially on my friend's cool IBM Selectric typewriter (he was still hunting and pecking his way through college English—evidently his mother had typed his debate cards for him, if you can believe it). Eventually I stumbled into a career path that requires me to type—a lot—and I live in a computerized world in which typing . . . er, keyboarding isn't just a handy skill—it's a matter of survival.

Now, I'm not saying Mom foresaw all of that when she refused to type my debate cards. Mostly, she wasn't willing to do something for me that I could do for myself. But in saying "no" to one small thing in high school, she actually said "yes" to a lot of big things in my life.

Whether or not I became a great typist.

Whose Plan Is It, Anyway?

Three sisters, six brothers, and a loving mother surrounded Laura last Friday evening. That's hardly surpris-
ing; the family had been planning for weeks to rally
around her participation in the state Junior Miss
Pageant. They planned on watching her compete. Okay,
let's be honest; they planned on watching her win.

But they hadn't planned on watching her die.

That's because the illness—a bacterial form of
meningitis—came upon her so quickly and devastated
her so completely. On Wednesday she went shopping
with her sister Chrissie. They had a great time together
making last-minute pageant preparations, and then they
stayed up late talking and laughing, with a little crying
thrown in for good measure. The only blot on an otherwise glorious day was a headache that Laura couldn't

seem to shake. But she shrugged it off, attributing it to a flu bug she had been battling or maybe pre-pageant jitters.

By midnight, however, she could no longer shrug off the headache. The pain increased to the point that it was beyond anything she had ever experienced, and she asked to be taken to the hospital emergency room. The nature of her illness was quickly diagnosed and treatments begun immediately. But it was already too late. Within a few hours she was in a coma. By 2:00 A.M. Friday she was no longer able to breathe for herself. By nine o'clock Friday morning, there was no evidence of brain activity. By noon Friday a doctor was soberly telling Laura's family that she wasn't going to survive and that they needed to begin thinking about when to remove the life support system and whether or not Laura would want to be an organ donor.

It all seemed surreal. Except for all the tubes and wires that were attached to her in the hospital intensive care unit, she didn't look sick. She looked like . . . well, like a girl who was ready to participate in a beauty pageant: tan, trim, great hair, manicured nails, and teeth that were whiter and straighter than teeth have a right to be. Just two days earlier she had been laughing with her sister, playing with her nieces, making jokes, and loving life.

And now, just like that, her life was over. The doctors said the bacteria normally isn't fatal but that for some unknown reason it will occasionally run roughshod over someone. Why Laura fell into that category nobody knows for sure. It's almost as if God, the Eternal Parent, called and said, "Young lady, it's time for you to come home now."

And Laura, ever the obedient child, responded.

Her family—six brothers, three sisters, and a loving mother—surrounded her hospital bed as the life-support equipment was turned off and Laura began a journey far more intimidating than a few steps on a pageant runway.

"Someday," said her tearful big sister Julie, "someday I'll understand."

Someday she will. Someday we'll all understand a lot of things that are incomprehensible to us from the limited perspective of here and now. Why must children suffer? Why does evil occasionally triumph over all that is right and noble? Why must bad things sometimes happen to good people? Why did Laura—young, beautiful, talented Laura, with a good heart, a kind soul, and a mind that suggested all the potential in the world—have to die? Why? Why? Why?

For now, instead of satisfying answers, we cling to faith. Faith in God. Faith in His love for all His children. And faith in His plan for our ultimate happiness and peace.

Especially when His plan goes contrary to our plans.

The Most Sacred Place on Earth

Every fall the builders and mortgage companies in our area sponsor what they call a Parade of Homes. This is not a parade in the traditional sense. They don't put a bunch of houses on floats and march them up and down the street. Rather, people march from house to house to look at the latest in home styles, floor plans, furnishings, and other assorted features.

This is one of Anita's favorite things to do. She says she's gathering ideas for decorating the house we will one day build. She loves to dream about that house. That's probably why we call it "the dream house." She's got it all planned, right down to the last screw in the last piece of drywall. The only thing she hasn't figured out yet is how to get the money to pay for it.

I, on the other hand, enjoy the Parade of Homes for another reason: if I'm good and don't whine too much while Anita drags me from house to house to house, she lets me pick out which fast food restaurant we go to for dinner. This year, I even learned a few things while dutifully—and non-whiningly—marching in the Parade:

• Mauve is out, sage is in (I am saddened by this, not because I have an affinity for mauve, but because I have finally figured out what color mauve actually is; sage, on the other hand, is . . . well, it's not mauve).

• There is no way to delicately describe the use and function of a bidet to an inquisitive 7-year-old boy (we finally settled on "it's a little sink to spit in"—this lie will, of course, be the one bit of instruction from his youth that he will actually remember, and it will probably lead to an international incident fifty years from now when he is ambassador to France. By then, with any luck, I'll be dead.)

• Believe it or not, there is such a thing as too much house (especially if the predominant decorative color in said house is red).

• Every house should have the following cool stuff

built right in: a spiral slide, a bathroom magazine rack, an aquarium wall, a lap pool, a vacuum, and a home theater system larger than the one at the local multiplex.

⋆ No matter how big or fancy or fully loaded the house is, there's still no place like home.

This last point became clear to me as we returned home from a full day of parading through houses. We had seen some lovely places, including one that . . . well, what's the next level beyond a dream house? An obsessive-compulsive house? These were great houses, filled with incredible furnishings and enhanced with magnificent landscaping. And yet as we pulled into the driveway of our cute little house, with its well-worn carpet, too-small kitchen, leaky plumbing, and not-quite-green-not-quite-brown (hey, it's sage!) lawn, I knew I was where I belong, and I was glad to be home.

Few concepts are so sweetly significant to humans as the concept of home. Whether we live in a showplace or a shanty, our home is at the heart of our most profound experiences, good and bad. As children, we are shaped and molded in the home and then sent out to build homes of our own. As parents, we try to make a good home for our children, knowing perfectly well that it will never be good enough, or strong enough, or safe enough, or secure enough. We build the best home we can—physically, spiritually, emotionally—we furnish it with love and then we pray that God will make up the difference. Our homes are therefore sanctified by our work, our love, our tears and our prayers. That's what makes it the most sacred place on earth.

With or without the parade.

"It's Good to Be Here"

A gentle autumn breeze ruffled my father's white, whispy hair. The rugged mountains behind him, resplendent in their fall colors, framed his face in vivid reds, golds, and yellows. He squinted his one good eye against the bright midday sunshine.

And he smiled.

I'd like to be able to tell you what he was smiling about. It could have been the fresh air, or the sunshine, or the fact that there was tapioca pudding waiting for him back inside the care center. It could have been any of them. Or all of them. Or none of them. We'll never know. Alzheimer's doesn't allow for a lot of explanation.

So we sat there, Dad in his wheelchair and I on a park bench, holding hands, and looking out over a pleasant, peaceful October morning. I asked him how he was feeling and he said, "Fine." I asked if the people at the care center were taking good care of him and he said, "Yes." I told him about the birth of my second granddaughter and how we are anxiously awaiting the arrival of another grandchild in March.

And he smiled.

At last I stood to begin the walk back to the care center. As I stooped to release the brakes on Dad's wheelchair, he reached up with a shaky hand and touched my cheek. I looked into his eyes. They were focused. Concentrated. He struggled to speak.

"It's . . . it's . . . good . . ."

I wasn't sure whether to wait and let him finish or to try to help him. During the last year or two, his ability to communicate had diminished significantly. I can't remember the last time I heard him utter a coherent sentence of more than a word or two. And yet, he seemed to be working so hard to say something. I had to help.

"What's good, Dad? The weather? The park? The care center? What's good?"

He seemed to gather himself for one last push.

"Here," he said. "To . . . be . . . here."

His struggle ended. His message was out there. But what was it?

"It's good to be here?" I asked. "Is that what you're trying to say? It's good to be here?"

And he smiled.

I took his frail hands in mine and kissed him on the forehead.

"Yes, it is, Dad," I said, tears surging to my eyes. "It's good to be here."

I considered his message as we strolled back to the care center. If any man has a right to complain about his current lot in life, it is my father. He led a good and honorable life, filled with love, service, and sacrifice. To be suffering the indignities of this disease at a time when he should be savoring the fruits of his labors seems patently unfair. And yet, in that one moment of clarity and comprehension, his one thought is that—despite everything—"it's good to be here."

I've thought about that in relation to my own life lately, and I've decided that Dad, as usual, is right. Despite the struggles, fears, and challenges that daily surround us, it's good to be here. It's good to be alive. It's good to experience all that life offers—the good things and the bad, the triumphs and the tragedies, the joys and the vicissitudes. It's good to be here even when it's bad to be here, because that's when we learn and grow the most.

I tried to explain all of that to Dad the next time I saw him.

And he smiled.

Treasures in the Sandbox

It was the first day of second grade, and Sarah was ready.

And why not? She had been looking forward to this moment since . . . well, since the last day of first grade.

Now that she wasn't a little baby first grader anymore she was anxious to take her place among The Big Kids. So of course it was important that everything be just so. She got the world's coolest backpack, complete with matching pencils and loose-leaf binders. She had her hair trimmed to a shorter, more mature length. And she bought some stylin' school clothes, including a killer outfit that featured khakis, a hot yellow shirt, and these really neat shoes that were sort of like tennis shoes, only they weren't, and they had buckles and . . . well, you just had to see them, that's all.

Mom helped to get the first day of school off to a great start by making Sarah's favorite breakfast—French toast. Only Sarah sort of dribbled syrup on her hot yellow shirt and stylin' khakis, so she had to run upstairs to change into her second-best outfit, consisting of blue jeans and a Disney Princess tee shirt—nice, but not killer.

The last-minute change put her way behind schedule, and the school bus was beginning to pull away from the curb as she rounded the corner. She dashed to catch the bus and was just reaching to pound on the door when the bus driver saw her, stopped the bus, and flung open the door—right in Sarah's face. Blood dripped from her nose onto her second-best outfit, and tears streamed from her now-blackened eyes as the chagrined bus driver tried to soothe and calm her.

"Maybe we should take you home, sweetheart," she said as she dried Sarah's tears.

"No!" Sarah insisted. "I'm okay. Let's go to school!"

They did their best to mop the blood off of Sarah's face and clothes, and they chugged off to school. Sarah was so excited to see her friends that she forgot all about

the morning's calamities. Since there were still a few minutes until school started she went to her favorite swing
on the playground and pumped herself to heights she
had never been able to achieve as a mere first-grader. At
the apex of her swing she saw her best friend across the
schoolyard. At precisely the wrong moment she let go of
the swing with one hand to wave. She flew out of the
swing and landed—hard and awkwardly—on the playground sand, breaking a leg and spraining a wrist. As she
lay in the sand, slowly drifting out of consciousness,
she noticed a shiny object on the ground not far from her
head. With her good hand she grabbed it. Then she
blacked out.

After being summoned by the school nurse, Sarah's
Mom rushed into the sick room to pick up her daughter.
She was stunned by what she saw: a sweet second grader
with her arm in a sling, her leg in a splint, a swollen nose,
two black eyes, and blood stains on her second-best
outfit. But what really troubled her was what was on
Sarah's face: the biggest, brightest smile you ever saw.

"Sarah, look at you!" her mother wailed. "You're
bruised, bandaged, and bloodied, and you've probably

ruined your second-best outfit. Why on earth could you possibly be smiling?"

"Look, Mommy," Sarah exclaimed, extending a still-sandy palm. "I found a quarter!"

School, like life, can be like that. It can be tough—even painful at times. But there are always treasures in the sandbox that make the challenges worth overcoming and the pain worth enduring.

On the first day. And every day.

The Allure of "Right Now"

A few years ago I tried an experiment with a group of ten-year-olds I was teaching in Sunday School.

"You have a choice," I announced as I held up a bowl of M&M's. "You can either have a handful of M&M's right now, or you can each have an entire bag of M&M's tomorrow."

"Why don't we do it the other way around?" Brady suggested. "Give us a bag of M&M's now or a handful tomorrow!"

The rest of the class loved Brady's idea. But I didn't.

"Nope," I said. "A handful now or the bag tomorrow. That's the way it's going to be."

"How about just a few now AND the rest later?" Megan asked.

"Sorry," I said. "No compromise. You have to make a choice."

"What if some of us want our M&M's now, and some of us want to wait?" Adam asked.

"Good idea," I said. "But no. Whatever you're going to do, you're going to do it as a group. You guys figure it out. I'm going to get a drink."

With that I stepped into the hall and wandered down to the drinking fountain, making sure to pause and stretch and meander. I wanted to give them plenty of time to hash this out. We were, after all, talking about chocolate here. If there's one thing twenty-nine years of marriage has taught me it's that you have to be very careful about decisions involving chocolate—even if it's the kind that melts in your mouth, not in your hands.

When I finally poked my head back into the room the decision had been made: the bowl of M&M's was empty, and there were chocolate-induced smiles all around.

"Actually, it was pretty much a no-brainer," Nancy said of the decision. "The hardest part was figuring out how to divide them up. The boys wanted to go first, but we didn't want to take a chance on the boys actually touching the M&M's before we got them. You never know where boys' hands have been—you know?"

Nancy, I should mention, has brothers.

So one of the boys—out of respect for delicate feelings, I won't say whose—arm-wrestled Nancy for the right to go first. I didn't see the actual event, but I'm confident the end came surely and swiftly. Think "Harry Potter Meets Xena, Warrior Princess." A battle of wits would have been competitive, but this wasn't about brain power. This was about brute strength.

Advantage Nancy.

The next day when I came home from work, several of the kids from my class were hanging out on my front lawn.

"We were just sort of thinking that . . . you know . . . maybe we should have waited to get a whole bag of M&M's today," Brady said. "And we were sort of wondering . . . you know . . . if it is, like, too late to change our minds?"

I smiled. "Yeah, it is," I said. "Sorry!"

"But the girls ate most of the M&M's in the bowl," Colton complained. "We hardly got any."

"That's too bad," I said. "If you had waited, not only would you have received more M&M's today than you got yesterday, but you would have received your own bag and you wouldn't have had to worry about how to divide them. But you decided not to wait, so you're pretty much stuck with what you got."

They didn't like that answer, but it brought new insight to our Bible class the next Sunday when we talked about how important it is to always stay focused on our ultimate, long-term goals and priorities no matter how alluring and intoxicating the diversions of Right Now may be.

You know, the story of Jacob, Laban, Leah, Rachel—and the M&M's.

Golden Guy

I wasn't asking much from my football career. I didn't expect to be Gale Sayers or Bart Starr or Jim Brown. I just wanted to be Kim Nelson.

Kim was one of the stars of my Pee-Wee Little League football team. He could do anything. He was quick. He was fast. He was strong. He could run the ball or he could throw it. He had a knack for making the big defensive play, and whenever we needed a touchdown Kim was just the guy to get it. And he did it often enough that we won the league championship.

Everyone on the team received a championship trophy. I couldn't help but notice that the little golden guy on top of the trophy looked a lot like Kim.

Not that I was jealous or anything.

Well, okay. Maybe I was a little jealous. The way I

saw it, the only advantage Kim had over me—I mean, besides superior athleticism, looks, personality, and talent—was size. He was smaller and lighter, which of course meant that he would be quicker and faster, right? But since I was taller and heavier I figured that meant I would be tougher to bring down. I dominated neighborhood football games because it always took three or four little guys to tackle me.

But I never got the chance in Pee-Wee league. I was a big guy, which meant only one thing to my coach: offensive line. So I spent the entire season blocking for Kim on his gallops to glory. Oh, I did have one sweet moment when the ball actually touched my hands. We were running a sweep to my side of the field, and I was out in front of Kim blocking. All of a sudden, I heard everyone yelling "Fumble!" at about the same time I felt the ball hit me in the back of my legs. I turned around to look for the ball just as it took one of those weird football bounces right up into my arms. I was so stunned and excited that I just sort of stood there.

"Run!" someone shouted from the sideline. "Run!"

Well, duh! Of course I knew I was supposed to run.

I wasn't stupid. I just didn't know which direction I was supposed to go. By the time I finally decided, a couple of players from the other team crashed into me, knocking the ball loose. Thankfully, someone from my team was in just the right place to pounce on the fumble and recover it for us.

You'll never guess who that someone was.

"Way to be alert out there, Kim!" the coach shouted.

Oh, and he had a few choice words for me, too: "Fall on the ball . . . what's his name again? Walker? Fall on the ball, Walker! Don't try to pick it up! You're not a ball-carrier!"

It was at about that point that I decided to leave the glory stuff to Kim. He was better at it than I was. Besides, I figured I could block for him better than he could block for me. And blocking is important—if not especially glamorous. The way I saw it, the face on the trophy may have been Kim's, but the ankles were definitely mine.

Ever since then, I've felt a special affinity for the non-ball-carriers among us—and not just in athletics. In every walk of life there are those who do the dirty work for those who get the glory. Homemakers, laborers, secretaries, paralegals, nurses, tellers, and all manner of assistants may not be the first people you think of during any discussion of society's movers and shakers. But without these folks behind the scenes, there is no moving, and precious little shaking.

No matter whose face is on the little golden guy.

The Power of Love

By any standard of measurement David was a powerful man.

Tall, handsome, and dignified, he cut an imposing figure, even in his declining years. He was widely known and greatly respected by his peers and others in the community. As the head of a large organization, he was surrounded by people who were prepared to respond to his every whim. Because of the prominence of his position and the value of his time, he didn't have to do anything that he didn't want to do or that wasn't a high priority for him.

Which is why it seemed a little unusual to those who worked in the small downtown market to see this great white-haired man, slowed and bent by the years, shuffling in to shop.

"Doesn't he have people to shop for him?" a clerk asked the store manager.

"Of course he does," the manager whispered. "He has people who have people who have people to do this sort of thing for him."

They watched as David moved slowly, deliberately, toward the produce section.

"Then what's he doing here?" the clerk asked.

"I don't know," the manager said, a little nervously. "But whatever it is, it must be VERY important."

David paused at the produce section, looking at the expansive display of fresh fruits and vegetables. At last his eyes settled on a bin of large, shiny red apples. He picked up the apples one by one, examining each closely, twisting and turning it in the sunlight to expose any defect or flaw. Over the course of several minutes he must have inspected two dozen apples or so until at last he settled on one that looked absolutely perfect— perfectly sized, perfectly shaped, perfectly colored, perfectly ripe.

"Perfect!" he said to himself, smiling broadly.

He tucked the apple securely in his hand and made

his way back up the aisle to the cash register, where the manager stepped in front of the clerk.

"There will be no charge for that, sir," the manager said when David presented the apple for purchase. "You may have it, with our compliments."

David shook his head.

"Thank you, sir," he said kindly. "But I insist. Please allow me to pay for this beautiful apple."

Reluctantly, the manager rang up the charge for the apple and placed it carefully in a brown paper bag. He took David's money, and handed the bag to him.

"Thank you," David said, holding the bag as one might hold a package of diamonds. "Emma will love this!"

Emma?

Of course—Emma. The love of David's life. His sweetheart of more than fifty years. It was said that in all their time together they had never once had an argument. And now, a clerk and a manager at a small downtown market understood why. It was a matter of priority. It was a matter of sensitivity. It was a matter of purpose. And clearly, it was a matter of power.

The power of love.

Wisdom with a Gold Star

Joe Jr. is in his first year at a prestigious law school in the eastern United States. A lot of folks are impressed by that.

But not Becky.

Becky is Joe's 5-going-on-35-year-old daughter. She has been in kindergarten for two whole months, which means she's pretty much got life figured out now.

For example, it didn't take her long to notice that she was the only one in her entire kindergarten class whose daddy still goes to school. All of the other daddies had jobs, including daddies who work on computers, daddies who build things, daddies who sell things, and even one daddy who is a police officer.

When you're in kindergarten, having a daddy who is

a police officer is prestigious. A daddy who is still going to school is . . . well . . . not.

"She hasn't said anything, but I can tell by the way she looks at me that she feels kind of sorry for me," Joe told me recently. "Most people think I'm in this law school because I'm smart. My daughter thinks I'm in this law school because I'm an idiot."

Which shouldn't come as a great surprise to Joe— pretty much all children see their fathers as idiots at some point in their lives. And they love us anyway. Most of the time.

The thing that really seals the deal for Becky is the stars. Every day in kindergarten the children earn gold stars for their behavior. The more gold stars on their paper at the end of the day, the better behaved they were. Usually Becky comes home with four or five stars on her paper. So when Joe brought one of his papers home from law school, she wanted to see it.

It may surprise you to learn that one of America's leading law schools doesn't normally put gold stars on student papers. So there were no stars on Joe's paper for Becky to see.

Joe could see the realization dawning in Becky's eyes. Not only was her father an idiot, but he was an idiot who behaved poorly. Becky looked at her father sadly and compassionately, as one might look at someone to whom life has done a great disservice.

"It's okay, Daddy," she soothed, patting his hand sympathetically. "I'll get a good job."

And as far as Becky is concerned, that's all right. The way she sees it, she's got kindergarten under control. Law school and the rest of life can't be any more difficult than that, can it?

Of course, those of us who have lived more than five years on this planet understand that there's a little more to it than that. Though it may be true, as Robert Fulghum's wonderful book indicates, that "Everything I need to know I learned in kindergarten," there is much to be said for the things we learn—sometimes painfully—through years of living and experience.

We may learn in kindergarten, as Fulghum writes, that you should "say you're sorry when you hurt somebody." But it is only through years of experiencing the pain of hurting and being hurt that we learn why that's such a good, healthy, healing idea. Or we may learn in kindergarten that we should "play fair." But we have to see and experience the consequences of unfairness to truly understand why playing fair is so important.

"Not all learning comes from books," said country music superstar Loretta Lynn. "You have to live a lot."

It's called wisdom, and you don't learn it at school—not even at the most prestigious of law schools. You don't even learn it at kindergarten, although some of it probably starts there. It rarely comes quickly or easily. But it comes in powerful ways that you never forget.

With or without the gold stars.

Redeeming the Christmas Villain

He's the great villain of Christmas. Check any Christmas pageant—you'll see.

He's the one played by the big, intimidating kid. I know this because that big, intimidating kid used to be me. And I played this guy so often I had the part down cold.

Which is exactly what the part calls for: Coldness. Aloofness. Indifference. Apathy.

You stand there with your arms crossed, looking ornery (and who wouldn't be ornery? You're standing there wearing your dad's bathrobe and a towel on your head). It's like you're just waiting to bark at someone (especially if anyone makes a crack about the towel). Sure enough, along comes the handsome boy (why couldn't I ever be the handsome boy?) and the cute girl with long dark hair (WHY COULDN'T I EVER BE THE HANDSOME BOY???) with the pillow stuffed under her robe to make her look . . . you know . . . "great with child."

You are the Innkeeper, and they are coming to you for lodging. Your job in the pageant is to turn them away rudely and to send them out into the stable to have their child. This I used to do with great flair, fixing the young couple with a steely glare, waving my arms wildly ("Oy vey! It's the middle of the tourist season, and you think you can just walk in here and get a room? What do you think this is, Inn 6?") and then pointing them toward the stable as the children's chorus behind us begins sweetly singing "Away in a Manger."

And then I would disappear. End of story. At least, it's the end of the Innkeeper's story.

Or is it?

Perhaps I grew too fond of the old boy by playing him for so many years, but I like to think of the Innkeeper wandering into the stable that first Christmas night. I see him standing in the shadows, watching in wonder and awe as angels herald the birth of a king. I think of him joining the shepherds at the side of the manger, falling to his knees to worship and adore. And I imagine him leaving his stable on Christmas morning a changed man—still big and intimidating, but somehow kinder and more compassionate.

And why not? One of the things I've learned through fifty or so Christmases is that the spirit of Christmas is a redemptive spirit. And not just in a theological sense. Look at our favorite Christmas stories:

• A miser is redeemed when ghostly visitors show him scenes from Christmases past, present, and future (or at least the future that will surely come if he doesn't change his ways);

• A bankrupt and suicidal building and loan company owner is redeemed when an angel (second class) shows him how much worse life would have been for the people he loves most if he hadn't been born;

• A green grinch is redeemed (and his heart grows three sizes) when the Whos refuse to give up the Christmas spirit despite the disappearance of all of their gifts (including the roast beast);

• A red-nosed reindeer is redeemed when inclement weather forces a toy cartel to seek an alternate lighting source for its annual overnight distribution run.

Clearly, the anecdotal evidence suggests that Christmas is about redemption through change: changing ideas, changing perceptions, changing relationships, changing values. But mostly, it's about changing self. And if that can apply to an English miser, a bankrupt and suicidal building and loan company owner, a green grinch, and a red-nosed reindeer, then surely it can apply to large, intimidating Innkeepers.

And the people who play them.

Love Squared

We had our own miracle last Christmas Eve.

Like the first Christmas miracle, ours was a miracle of birth. Only our miracle didn't take place in a stable; it happened in a modern, state-of-the-art hospital. Instead of a manger filled with straw, our Christmas baby lay down her sweet head in a comfortably warm, carefully sterilized bassinet. And while there were no cattle or shepherds to attend the birth of our precious little one, there were plenty of nurses, grandparents, aunts, uncles, and cousins.

Not to mention the wise man/doctor occasionally poking a head in. From the east, as I recall.

Now, I know there are tens of thousands of births every day on this planet, and there was nothing that made our experience any more "miraculous" than any other. But for me, it was a magical moment of transformation. Before my very eyes, my son became a father, my wife became a grandmother, my daughters became aunts, my youngest son became an uncle, and that basketball in my daughter-in-law's tummy became The World's Most Adorable Granddaughter.

Miraculously.

There were some extraordinary moments during that long and . . . well, almost sacred Christmas Eve. No, we didn't have herald angels harking in the heavens, or a new star overhead to light the way to baby Becky. But we did have an eight-year-old Jon excitedly telling everyone: "I'm an uncle! I'm an uncle!" We had two grandmothers—one a veteran, one a first-timer—taking turns monitoring the hospital staff to make sure they were taking proper care of "their" granddaughter. And we had two families coming together at the nursery window to "ooh!" and "ahh!" at the little dark-haired bundle in the bassinet who represented their confluence.

For me, however, the most profound moments involved my son: the joy in his eyes as he held up his daughter for all the family to see; the tender concern etched on his face as he oversaw the poking and probing and assorted testing of little Becky; and the peaceful contentment that emanated from him as he sat in a hospital rocking chair holding his sweet, slumbering child.

I had gone to get him some food—hey, a guy's gotta eat, even on Christmas Eve—and I brought it to the hospital room where the new little family was headquartered. New Mama Jenny was resting comfortably, and Joe was holding Becky. For a moment, I stood silently and watched my son gently cradle his baby in his long, powerful arms. At first, all I could see was the top of Joe's head as he bent to her, examining her, studying her, kissing her little hands and cheeks. Then he looked up at me, and I could see the tears that were streaming down his face.

"You were right," he said as a tear dripped from his cheek and fell softly on Becky's hand.

I hesitated. I had lectured Joe about so many things through the years I wasn't exactly sure which thing I had been right about. "I was?" I asked.

He glanced down at Becky, then back at me. "This . . . this . . . feeling," he said. "I've never felt anything like it. It's like . . . love . . . squared. To the Nth degree."

I understood. I was feeling that same feeling for my child—and my grandchild. And it made me think that perhaps that is truly the essence of Christmas. It's not just about a child, and it's not just about parents—heavenly or otherwise. It's about love.

Squared.

Miraculously.

Random Acts of Curmudgeon-ness

Go ahead. Look up the word *curmudgeon* in the dictionary. You'll see. There's no definition there. Just a picture of Dan.

Dan isn't a bad guy. Not at all. He's a good guy, actually. His benevolence and generosity are well-known. Professionally, he has a great reputation in a field where reputation is everything. He's a pro's pro, and has been for many years. But he's sort of . . . well, crusty. And churlish. And cantankerous.

You know—curmudgeonly.

That's why Lindsey hesitated a moment before taking the seat next to him on the shoe-shine stand. She and Dan have often worked together on various projects, and they always get along just fine. Still, he intimidates her—partly because she respects him so much, and partly because of . . . well, you know . . . the c-word.

But an early winter storm had taken its toll on her shoes, and she had a big presentation to make—the kind that makes you grasp for any edge you can find, including clean, shiny shoes. So she climbed into the chair next to Dan, and for the next few minutes they chatted. No, that's not quite right—for the next few minutes Lindsey chatted self-consciously, and Dan grunted every now and then. He wasn't being rude or anything. He was just being Dan.

You know—curmudgeonly.

When Dan's shoes were done, he inspected them carefully and spoke quietly but firmly to the shoe shine proprietor as he paid his bill. Then he bid Lindsey a terse good-bye and was gone—much to Lindsey's relief. She relaxed while the rest of her shoeshine was completed and tried to gather her thoughts for her presentation. When her shine was finished, she stepped down from the chair and reached into her purse for her wallet.

"No need for that, ma'am," the shoe shiner said,

smiling. "That gentleman who was here before—he already paid for your shoeshine."

"He what?" Lindsey was dumbfounded.

"He paid for yours when he paid for his. Nice guy, huh?"

The kindness of Dan's gesture brought a smile to Lindsey's face—and to her heart. She went to her presentation feeling happy, buoyant, and full of confidence. Not surprisingly, it went remarkably well. In fact, everything seemed to go better for her that day—and not just because she had such nice, shiny shoes.

A few days later Lindsey was standing in line at a mall eatery when she noticed a ruckus in front of her. A young mother with several restless children had come up short of change and was rummaging through her purse hoping to find money to pay for the food she had ordered. Her children were crying, and she appeared to be near tears herself until Lindsey stepped forward, paid the missing balance (interestingly, almost exactly the same amount her shoe shine would have cost), and helped the frazzled woman and her family get their meal to a table. When the grateful lady asked for her name and address so she could pay her back the money, Lindsey told her not to worry about it.

"By helping you, I'm paying back someone who did something nice for me," she said. "If you want to pay me back, you're going to have to find someone else to help."

And she almost looked . . . you know . . . curmudgeonly when she said it.

Dunking Mike

Our family basketball games changed when Mike started playing.

Which, come to think of it, could be taken any number of ways, since there are no fewer than nine Mikes in the family, and they all play basketball to one degree or another. The Mike to whom I am referring is one of the most recent Mikes—a 6-foot, 8-inch former college-basketball-playing Mike who married into the family a couple of years ago. As with all the other family Mikes, this Mike is a good guy. But this Mike can also dunk.

And that changes everything.

Suddenly everyone on the floor started working a little bit harder to elevate their game. Dunking Mike was pretty cool about being bigger and better than everyone else. He actually toned down his game a bit, but he still dominated on both ends of the floor. The games became a lot more competitive and intense as all the former high school basketball players (and high school shoulda-beens) worked to prove that they belonged on the same court with Dunking Mike.

And that made for some interesting games. Fun games. Competitive games.

Maybe a little TOO competitive.

During one recent game, things started getting heated. Now, you've got to understand something about our family games. When we get mad, we don't get mad at each other—we get mad at ourselves. Our minds remember what we are supposed to do, but our bodies have forgotten. And so we get frustrated with ourselves, and occasionally we express that frustration verbally. We say: "Goodness gracious! I'm playing poorly! I need to move with more precision and vigor!"

Or words to that effect.

On this particular day, some words were spoken that sounded unduly harsh. Profane, in fact. And my son Jon, the youngest of the hooping cousins, was bothered by them. Not that he'd never heard such language. Sadly, he hears it all the time at school. It's just that he'd never heard it from his close family. And so he came home from the game that day a little disillusioned to think that one of the guys he looked up to—literally and figuratively—would use language like that. And I wasn't exactly sure what to tell him. On the one hand, I didn't want to justify the use of profanity. But on the other hand, I didn't want to condemn a group of young men who I love and who were, in every other respect, outstanding role models for my son.

Thankfully, Dunking Mike knew how to elevate his game. Only this time it wasn't with a dunk or a blocked shot. This time it was with an e-mail addressed specifically to Jon.

"I just wanted to write a little apology for what was said during Saturday's basketball game," wrote Dunking Mike three days after the game. "I don't know who said it, buddy, but I want you to know it wasn't me. Sometimes things slip out and people say things that they shouldn't. I understand that. But it's important to me that you know that I didn't swear.

"Jon, swearing is wrong, and when people do it they

are not setting a good example," Dunking Mike continued, "I apologize on behalf of all of us. As your older cousins, we need to set a good example for you to follow. And I promise from now on we will."

There have only been a couple of family basketball games since that day. But so far, Dunking Mike has made good on his promise.

And that's a slam dunk any way you look at it.

Prosperity, Honestly Earned

Every year in Cub Scout Pack 509 we held a Pinewood Derby.

And every year I lost.

By "lost" I don't mean that I finished second or third. No, sir. I mean I finished last. Dead last. And not a close last. Not a respectable last. Not a competitive last. I was last by a mile. Way last. I was to Pinewood Derby racing what Harold Stassen was to politics.

A loveable loser.

But a loser nonetheless.

For the uninformed, a Pinewood Derby is a diabolical little contest involving boys, dads, a little block of pine, and a steep, wooden racing track. The object of the event is for boys to work together with their dads to carve their block of pine into a little race car, and then to race these cars down the steep track against each other in a series of head-to-head matches to determine who has made the fastest car. According to my Scout leaders, the event was all about getting dads to spend time working on an interesting project with their boys. But to me and my fellow Cubs, it was all about winning.

Especially when you lost.

That's why I was intrigued when, just before my third and final Pinewood Derby, a friend at school said he knew a sure-fire way to win. I begged him for details, and he complied.

"But isn't that cheating?" I asked when he explained the procedure.

"Well, technically, yes," he said. "But that's the only way your car will win."

He had a point there. As father and son, Dad and I were terrific. We got along great, and enjoyed working together on the project. But as car builders, we were . . . well, awful. I had serious doubts that the purple and black monstrosity we had constructed would make it all the way to the end of the track without falling apart, much less win any races. So on my own I made the decision to make the "adjustments" my friend proposed. I won't divulge any details of those adjustments here (in much the same way that I wouldn't provide a recipe for making an atomic bomb), and I won't tell you my friend's name because I'm not exactly sure when the statute of limitations expires for Pinewood Derby Fraud. But I cheated, pure and simple.

And I won.

I have to admit, it was kind of exciting to watch my little wooden car speeding down that ramp ahead of all comers, winning race after race in impressive fashion. Even my Dad seemed pleased—and a little surprised— at our sudden success. And when they placed that little gold trophy in my hands at the end of the evening, I was thrilled beyond words.

At least, I was until later that night, when I set my car and trophy on the prominent spot I had reserved for them on my dresser. I sat and stared at them, hoping to rekindle some of the excitement I felt earlier. I was a winner! So why did I feel like such a loser? The fact was, I hadn't earned that trophy honestly. I knew it. And that knowledge—coupled with the gnawing fear that at any time my friend at school could blow the whistle on my fraudulent foray into the winner's circle—dampened any joy I felt during the Pinewood Derby, and left me feeling empty and ashamed.

So I took the trophy and the car and buried them in my bottom drawer, where they remained until I threw them away a few years later.

Some people say that cheaters never prosper. I'm not sure that's true. Sometimes they do. But there's no lasting joy in prosperity that isn't honestly earned.

Even if it turns a loveable loser into a winner.

Christmas Sunday

For those who dream of a white Christmas, 1988 was a dream come true.

A winter storm dumped more than a foot of snow in our area early that Christmas Sunday morning. From the warmth and security of my living room it was a magnificent sight. The snow lay in a thick, powdery blanket that gave the roads, yards, and orchards outside the appearance of being joined together as one huge, flat, white field. Smoke curled out of brick chimneys that extended up through what seemed to be a thick layer of marshmallow rooftop frosting, giving every house a cozy Courier & Ives ornamentation. Tree boughs bent sharply beneath the heavy load of snow, and "the treetops glistened"—just like the song says.

It was picturesque—no question about it.

Until you tried to travel in it. Then all of that beautiful snow suddenly became an icy adversary that caused tires to spin and made roads impassable. All of which was fine for those who were inclined to spend a nice, quiet Christmas at home. But for those who planned on traveling "over the river and through the woods"—or even just a few blocks to attend church services—the snow presented a challenge of significant proportions.

It became clear to me just how significant those challenges would be when I tried to negotiate the two blocks to church on foot. Trudging through the deep snow was laborious, and I slipped frequently on patches of ice. As the lay leader of our local church congregation, I was concerned for those who would venture out to attend our Christmas worship service—especially those wonderfully faithful elderly couples and widows who always attended. No matter what.

When I got to the church I called Sam, my good friend and one of my associates in the lay ministry, and I suggested the possibility of canceling services because of the snow.

"Oh, we can't do that," he said. "It's Christmas!"

"But I don't know if it's safe . . ."

"Don't you worry about that," he said. "Everything will be fine. You'll see."

Buoyed by Sam's faith and assurance, I began preparing the church for worship. I turned on the lights, cranked up the heat in the chapel, set up a few extra chairs in the back (well, it WAS Christmas Sunday, after all), and then headed out to shovel the sidewalks. The snow was heavy and wet, and there was a ton of it to remove. There was no way I was going to get it all done before church. And I had no idea what to do about the parking lot, which was still covered with so much snow that it would be dangerous for cars pulling in and out.

Suddenly I heard a chugging sound slowly coming down the tree-lined lane leading up to the church. I knew that sound—it was George, a good-hearted member of our congregation. He was using the blade on his tractor to plow a path to church. He waved as he chugged into the parking lot and began clearing away snow for the cars that soon would be coming.

I bowed my head and silently thanked God for George. But when I looked up I realized I had much more for which to be grateful. A small army of men—old and young—armed with snow shovels were descending on the church sidewalks to finish the job I had barely started. In no time the walks were clean and the parking lot was ready for those who would drive to church.

I thanked George and the others for their help and gently suggested that we take a few minutes to dig out some of our elderly couples and widows.

"Too late," George said through the frost accumulating on his thick white moustache.

I looked at my watch. "We've got a half-hour. If we divide up I'm sure we can—"

"It's done," George interrupted. "Every house in the neighborhood. Merry Christmas!"

I looked at George and at the smiling faces of men and boys who had left their warm homes and Christmas presents to move a mountain of snow so that their neighbors could safely travel to worship—and I wept. There were no words to express what I was feeling and what they had taught me that Christmas Sunday. But as we stood there in that circle of service, noses running and cheeks pink from the cold, we were warm.

Because of effort. Because of love. But mostly, because of Christmas.

A Valentine for Grandma

It was just a harmless prank, that's all it was. And it wasn't as if Old Lady Hayes didn't deserve it. The way she used to scream at us for "borrowing" a few of her precious raspberries each summer, like we were stealing gold out of Fort Knox . . . well, she had it coming.

At least, that's the way we saw it as George finished tying the string to the red, heart-shaped box. We giggled as Ron added the final touch: two plastic red roses, glued to the lid. "I wonder what will surprise her most," I asked as George practiced jerking the box out of reach by yanking on the string. "Seeing a box of candy on her step, or watching it fly away when she tries to pick it up?"

We laughed as we watched George make Albert chase the box around the garage. For a chubby 10-year-old, Albert did a good imitation of Mrs. Hayes's hunched hobble and her seemingly permanent scowl. And we howled when he picked up a broom and pretended to ride it through the midwinter air while shouting, "I'm Old Lady Hayes, the driedest-up old prune in the West!"

Ron was first to notice my dad in the doorway. Within seconds, Ron's anxiety was shared by all but Albert, who continued to swoop around the garage until he came face-to-belt-buckle with our silent observer. For a moment the only movement in the room came from the little puffs of steam escaping our mouths. Dad broke the stillness by walking slowly to the empty candy box lying on the floor. He picked it up and dangled it by the string, watching it swing back and forth. Then he looked into the eyes of the frightened boys.

And, as was his custom, he looked into their hearts as well.

"It doesn't seem so long ago that I was pulling Valentine's Day pranks," he said as he laid the box on a workbench. "One year my cousins and I decided to pull one on our Grandma Walker even though we loved her. We were just feeling devilish and decided to have some fun at her expense.

"Early in the evening we snuck up to her doorstep with a can of red paint. Grandma was hard of hearing, so we didn't have to worry about being very quiet. Which was a good thing, because every time we thought about how funny it was going to be to see Grandma try to pick up a valentine that was just painted on her doorstep, we couldn't keep from laughing.

"It didn't take long, and it wasn't very artistic. But for an old woman with bad eyes, it would do. We kicked the door and hid behind bushes. When Grandma finally appeared she stood in the doorway, her gray hair pulled back tightly into her usual bun, wiping her hands on her usual apron. She must have heard the commotion in the bushes because she looked in our direction and spoke loudly enough for us to hear: 'Who could be knocking at my door?' Then she looked down. Even from fifteen feet away we could see the joy in her eyes when she spotted a splash of red at her feet.

"'Oh, look! A valentine for Grandma!' she exclaimed. 'And I thought I'd be forgotten again this year!'

"She tried to retrieve her prize. This was the moment we had been waiting for, but somehow it wasn't as much fun as we expected. Grandma groped at the fresh paint for a moment. Slowly, she figured out the prank. She tried to smile. Then, with as much dignity as she could muster, she turned and walked back into her house, absently wiping red paint on her white apron."

Dad paused, and for the first time I noticed that his eyes were moist. He took a deep breath. "Grandma died later that year," he said. "I never had another chance to give her a real valentine."

He took the box from the bench and handed it to me. Then he turned and left the garage.

Later that night a red, heart-shaped box with two plastic roses on it was placed on Mrs. Hayes's front doorstep by six giggling boys. We hid behind snow-covered bushes to see how she would react to receiving a full pound of candy and nuts.

With no strings attached.

Gratitude First

I'm not exactly sure why I gave the necklace to Kayla.

I had an extra necklace. Kayla was sitting in front of me at church. It just seemed like the thing to do.

Now, keep in mind that I'm talking about a candy necklace here—nothing special at all. It was just a stringy loop of elastic with multi-colored candies strung around it. I had handed some of them to the 10-year-olds to whom I have been teaching Old Testament stories for the past year (what, you don't see the connection between candy necklaces and the Old Testament?), and I had an extra one (well, actually I had an extra three, but my two youngest children, Jon and Elizabeth, were already wearing two of them around their respective necks, with candy fragments already glistening on their respective lips).

Kayla, on the other hand, is quite special indeed. She has long dark hair. Gorgeous eyes. A beautiful smile. The sweetest voice you've ever heard. And she's six. In all the world there is nothing so wonderfully adorable as a six-year-old girl.

Which is probably why I gave the necklace to her. I'm a sucker for that stuff.

When I slipped the necklace into her hand she smiled that beautiful smile of hers, and I considered myself adequately thanked. Then I settled back to enjoy the church meeting. As enthralling as church was that day, I did notice a couple of things about Kayla. For one thing, although she wore the candy necklace around her neck, I didn't see her actually eating the candy. By way of comparison, Jon had his necklace consumed and was asking for more before we sang the final "Alleluia" in the opening hymn.

The other thing I noticed was that she seemed quite intent on something she was drawing. I couldn't see it, but whatever it was it certainly had her attention—so much so that she paid almost no attention to the candy strung around her neck.

When the service ended I stood to leave. Then I noticed something small and cute in the aisle beside me. It was Kayla. She didn't say a word. She just handed a piece of paper to me. It was the picture that she had been working on throughout the meeting. It showed a tall stick figure man with glasses and most of his hair, holding a candy necklace in his hand. Next to him was a shorter stick figure girl with long dark hair, gorgeous eyes, and a beautiful smile. Over her head was a cartoon balloon with these words: "Thank you."

It was a lovely gift and a marvelous work of art—far more valuable than the candy bauble I had presented to her. As I thanked her for her gift, I noticed that she was finally starting to eat the candy that I had given to her.

"It looks like your Daddy wouldn't let you eat your candy until after church," I observed.

She shook her head seriously.

"I could eat it," she said, shyly. "I just wanted to say 'thank-you' first."

I was touched by her gesture and inspired by her message. It was so important to her to say "thank you" that she couldn't really enjoy the treat until she had expressed her gratitude.

That's why there's a new piece of art in the gallery that is beginning to fill the nooks and crannies of my office. Kayla's picture is the first to be so enshrined that wasn't created by one of my offspring. I'm including it as a way of reminding me to be grateful.

First.

Finding the Blessing
in the Curse

There is a place where modern technological conveniences go to die.

My place.

During the past week alone we have sent our van's fuel pump to the automotive afterlife, our washing machine to laundry Valhalla, and our home computer through those big Windows in the sky. They join the lifeless metallic hulks of our dishwasher, our microwave oven, and our food processor, all of which have given up the electronic ghost during the last few months.

If there were laws against appliance abuse, I'd be public enemy number one.

Thankfully, we do better with living things—not counting household plants, flowers, grass, and tomatoes.

Our five children somehow manage to survive—even thrive—despite all the bad feng shui and negative karma. They are all healthy, happy, and well-adjusted, give or take the occasional drama major. And that, after all, is what really matters.

At least, that's what my wife, Anita, said.

"This is just stuff," she said soothingly, reassuringly, as I wrote out a check to cover the installation of the new fuel pump.

"Yes it is," I said, my fingers still trembling. "Very expensive stuff. Do you realize that this fuel pump is costing me more than the first car I bought?"

She smiled playfully. "What a blessing!" she said.

I looked at her curiously. "A blessing?" I asked. "We just spent an entire freelance check on a fuel pump, and you think it's a blessing?"

"Uh-huh," she said. "What a blessing that we had the money to cover it!"

She had a valid point—as usual. But I couldn't let her win this easily. "What about losing the washing machine at the same time?" I asked. "Was that a blessing, too?"

"Sure," she said. "My brother feels good about letting us use his machine, and I'm able to spend a little more time with him and his family while I wash our clothes at his house. And I'm really going to appreciate our new washer when we get it."

She was good. No question about it. Twenty-three years of living with me had given her plenty of experience at searching for silver linings. But I knew I had her with the last one. "And what about our computer meltdown?" I asked. "What's the blessing in that?"

A worried look crossed her face. This was tough, no question about it. It's like they say: everyone makes mistakes, but it takes a computer to really foul things up.

Then, suddenly, she brightened.

"You're not staying up so late working on the computer," she said, "so you're getting a lot more sleep! That's a good thing, isn't it?"

She had me there. I had actually noticed how much better I had been feeling the past few days, and had already attributed it to getting more sleep.

"Okay, you win!" I said. "But how do you do that— finding the blessing in the curse?"

"It isn't hard, really," she said. "The blessing is always there—somewhere. You just have to look for it. Sometimes you have to look pretty hard. But it's there."

Even at my place.

Healing the Soul

It was only a fragment of conversation, a bit of disjointed syntax floating on the ether of multi-linguistic communication of an international airport the day after another heartbreaking "incident" garnered worldwide interest and concern.

I didn't even hear enough to be able to identify the accent, let alone the actual speaker. But I heard enough that I've been pondering the comment ever since.

"If there was a God," the voice said, "He wouldn't allow such things to happen. What's the point of praying to a god who lets people suffer? It's a joke. It's a farce. God is . . ."

I didn't hear the final declaration, but something tells me it was not a declaration of belief.

As a person of faith I am not offended by such

sentiments. I understand why it is difficult for some people to believe. But I am troubled. And saddened. And I can't help but wonder what Drexell Beckman would have said if he had been in that airport.

Drexell Beckman was the lay leader of our church congregation for several years. Then someone else took over the congregation, and Brother Beckman became Sunday School teacher to the biggest, baddest batch of 12- and 13-year-olds to ever tackle a Testament. There were twenty-five of us in the class, and we had a reputation for chewing up and spitting out those who tried to teach us. I remember one stretch during which we went through five or six teachers in about three months. We went through Sunday School teachers like Godzilla went through Tokyo.

It wasn't that we were completely unredeemable. It was actually, in retrospect, a pretty terrific group of young people. But there were so many of us. And we enjoyed being together, which meant we were very social. And, okay, I'll admit it—we boys were just discovering how great girls are, and we wanted to impress them. So we were constantly acting up and showing off, like the time

George got stuck in the window while trying to climb out of it.

No, wait. That was me. George was the one who snuck a puppy into Sunday School.

No, wait. That was me, too. But George did some bad stuff also. Trust me. He did.

We all did. So they split up the class—boys in one class, girls in another—and gave the boys to Drexell Beckman. And that was the end of the trouble. For one thing, the girls were in another class, so there was no point in showing off. For another, we all knew and loved Brother Beckman, and so he immediately commanded our attention and respect.

And for still another, his Sunday School lessons were powerful. He had a unique way of taking Bible stories and making them come to life. His love for the scriptures and for God was palpable, and he touched us with his conviction. He talked with us, not at us, about religion and how it applied to our lives in everyday ways.

One day, during a lesson about prayer, one of the boys asked about Nina Brinkerhoff. Nina was a member of our congregation who suffered greatly from illness. We often prayed for her during church meetings. If God is so powerful and loving, the boy wanted to know, why was Nina still sick?

The wise teacher looked at the floor for a moment as he considered his response. Finally he said: "Having faith doesn't mean that you won't ever have problems. We live in a world where there is illness, where there are tragic accidents, where disasters happen. And we live in this imperfect world with these fragile, imperfect bodies, so bad things can happen. Faith doesn't change that. But faith in God and in His eternal promises can give us the courage we need to be able to cope with illness, tragedy, and disaster when they happen."

He paused, then added: "That's what Nina's faith has done for her. It hasn't healed her body, but it has healed her soul. And for a person of faith, that's the most important thing."

No matter what you may have overheard at the airport.

Mom's Old Useless Bible

To tell the truth, I don't remember ever seeing Mom actually read her old Bible. As far as I could tell, it just sat on the nightstand next to her bed.

And that was the best place for it, since it probably wouldn't have survived any meaningful usage anywhere else. The black cloth cover was ragged and time-worn, its dog-eared pages yellowed with time. Once I accidentally knocked it off the nightstand, launching loose pages all over Mom and Dad's bedroom. I expected a tongue-lashing for my carelessness (and believe me, this was no small expectation, since Mom delivered a tongue-lashing like Pavarotti delivers an aria—with the practiced precision and stunning power of an artist). But Mom was so busy gathering the pages, gently smoothing them and returning them to their place in the book that she paid no attention to me.

Soon after I moved away from home my sister, Kathy, and I combined our funds to buy a new Bible for Mom for her birthday. It was a black leather volume, twice as big as her old Bible. The pages were trimmed in gold, and there were maps, references, and a complete Bible dictionary included within its cover. We even had her name engraved on the front with gold-leaf lettering.

It was a beautiful book, and Mom was both touched and pleased to receive it. I remember watching her thumb carefully through the pages, admiring the quality of the paper and the clarity of the printing. From that day on, it was the Bible she took with her to church, and the one from which she read during the family Nativity pageant. But for some reason, it never displaced the old Bible from its position of honor on her nightstand. And that kind of bothered me.

"I don't know why you keep that ratty old thing," I told her as we prepared to pack it among her most precious belongings for what would turn out to be the last of many relocations in her life—this time to the warm, heavy air of Southern California. "That new Bible we got for you is the best that money can buy. You can't even use this old one anymore."

Mom smiled at me weakly and sat on the edge of her bed, carefully wrapping the old Bible in an equally old, equally shabby white shawl.

"Just because a thing isn't useful anymore, that doesn't mean it isn't valuable," she said softly. "You look at this and see an old, worn-out book. But I see the gift your father gave me on our wedding day. I see the friend that was always there to provide strength and comfort when your father was sent to Pearl Harbor during the war. I see the storybook from which I read to all of my children, and the primer from which you all read your first Bible verses.

"This Bible has been in the family as long as we've been a family," she continued, caressing it through the tattered shawl. "It's part of us, part of our history, part of who we are. So even though it isn't especially useful anymore, there is still value in what it represents. At least, there is to me."

Suddenly it occurred to me that she wasn't just

talking about her old Bible. We live in an age of fanatically obsessive utilitarianism. Everything is disposable—even people. If it's old or odd-looking or not particularly useful, toss it—or him, or her—out. We forget that there is value beyond utility, and worth beyond "what's in it for me now."

When Mom died, Dad gave me her "new" Bible. It's among my most cherished possessions. It's the Bible I read and take to church. It means a lot to me, and it really is beautiful and incredibly useful. But I'd trade it in a minute for Mom's old, useless Bible.

I even have the perfect place for it: on the nightstand next to my bed.

Waiting for a Good Samaritan

My sister, Kathy, and Dad's wife, Jean, took our 87-year-old father to the doctor recently. The doctor asked if Dad had any difficulty getting out of a chair. Dad said, "No—no problems at all. I'm doing great!" Kathy and Jean looked at each other nervously, and then Jean cleared her throat and gently told the doctor that, yes, he does need assistance getting out of a chair.

Then the doctor asked if he ever fell or stumbled. Dad said, "No—I don't ever fall." Jean and Kathy looked at each other again, chuckling, and then Jean reported that he is frequently wobbly and falls fairly often.

Then the doctor asked if he needed any assistance in walking. "No," Dad said. "I'm doing just fine in walking." Jean interjected again, reporting that he does just fine as long as he uses two canes or if there's someone strong alongside to help hold him up.

The doctor smiled patiently. "I think I already know the answer to this next question," he said, "but how is your memory? Are you finding yourself forgetting things?"

"No, I don't have a problem with that at all," Dad said. Then he looked at Jean and asked: "Do I, Honey?"

In other words, situation normal with our ever-optimistic father. He thinks he's in great condition ... for someone in his condition. And he probably is. But that sort of begs the point, doesn't it? The fact is, age isn't creeping up on Dad; it has overtaken him and left him in the dust. But Dad has a hard time seeing it. He still thinks he's 70, which may sound old to most of us, but for Dad 70 was a walk in the park. Dad was a stud at 70—strong, active, alert, dynamic, energetic, vibrant. I'm in worse shape at 43 than Dad was at 70.

But Dad isn't 70 anymore. You don't have to spend much time with him to see that. He's sweet and wonderful and charming. But he can't do everything that he could do when he was younger. You know—like getting out of a chair. And walking. And remembering stuff. None of which is problematic for those of us who know and love him. It's just a problem when he tries to do things that he can't—or shouldn't—do anymore.

Like the other day when he awakened early and decided to go for a walk without telling Jean and without his canes. He got as far as the driveway outside his home before he fell, dislocating his finger and cutting his hand badly enough to require stitches. We don't know how long he was out there on his hands and knees, bleeding and unable to get up, before a Good Samaritan came along to help him back to the house (thank you, sir, whoever you are!). And we don't know if he really understands that he can't go for walks—caneless and alone—anymore, which means we are now in the uncomfortable position of having to limit his freedom so he doesn't hurt himself.

There's nothing quite as frightening as people who are unaware of their limitations: the toddler who thinks she can carry the baby up the stairs, the teenager who thinks he is invulnerable behind the wheel of the car, the middle-aged father who thinks he can keep up with his

18-year-old son on the basketball court, the second soprano who thinks she can hit the high notes in "The Star-Spangled Banner."

Just as it is important to know our strengths and cultivate our talents, we also need to be aware of our weaknesses. Sure, we can work on them, maybe even turn a few into strengths. But even then, we need to make sure we know when a weakness really has become a strength, or we may find ourselves on our hands and knees— bloodied, dislocated, and waiting for a Good Samaritan.

United We Stand

You can learn a lot from a horse.

Well, okay—maybe not a lot. I mean, I'm not suggesting anything Mr. Ed-ish here. No therapeutic thoroughbreds. No psychics in saddles. A horse is a horse.

Of course? Of course.

Still, there are things we can learn from horses. For example, I heard about a Canadian competition during which huge Clydesdale work horses are hitched to a special sled that allows weights to be added to measure the horse's strength. During the most recent competition the winning horse pulled about 8,000 pounds, while the second-place finisher pulled 7,000 pounds.

Hey, there's a reason we use the phrase "strong as a horse."

The competition also includes a team pulling event,

and it turned out that during this year's competition one of the teams consisted of the first- and second-place finishers from the individual pulling event. So it stands to reason that if you put them together, they should be able to pull about . . . wait a second . . . these are big numbers . . . using ALL my fingers and toes here . . . about 15,000 pounds, give or take a kilogram. Right?

Wrong.

Actually, when the two horses were hitched together they managed to pull a sled weighing 33,000 pounds—more than four times the amount each could pull individually!

I'm sure there's some scientific principle of physics that comes into play here—equine synergism, perhaps?—or some complex mathematical equation that would explain how such a thing happens. But that would doubtless require brilliant insight, thoughtful consideration, and at least two teenagers' worth of computer know-how, and you know perfectly well you're not going to get any of that here.

I prefer the explanation of an ancient teacher named Aesop (and no, he wasn't MY teacher—he was a little before my time, and I'm pretty sure he went to a different high school). This wise philosopher would use sticks to illustrate the point. He would hold up one stick and ask one of his listeners to break it—which could easily be done. Then he would hold up two sticks, and repeat the process. Then three, and so on until the little bundle of sticks couldn't be broken, no matter how hard his student tried.

"Alone, we are weak and easily broken," Aesop would explain, "but together, we are strong."

Abraham Lincoln tried to teach the same concept to a nation coming apart at the seams. "United we stand," said he, "divided we fall."

Or was it the 5th Dimension that said that? I always get them confused.

In any case, it's a significant concept for families, communities, church congregations, businesses, and nations. No matter how strong we may be individually, our strength is multiplied exponentially when we stand shoulder-to-shoulder, arm-in-arm, together with others.

But don't take my word for it. Go right to the source.

Ask a horse.

The "Thing" about Soft Answers

The day had been long and tiring, and I was looking forward to relaxing with the evening paper. But that was going to be impossible as long as Elizabeth and Jonathan were awake.

"Okay, guys," I said. "Bedtime."

Big sister Andrea tried to be helpful: "But isn't it a little early—?" I gave her one of my famous one-more-word-and-you-sleep-in-a-tree glances. "Oh, yeah," she continued. "Bedtime!"

So we did the bath thing, the teeth thing, the prayer thing, and the story thing. Hugs and kisses and "I love you's" were properly administered—twice. Warm covers were tucked under chins. Lights were turned off. The last "have a good sleep" was said, and I was on my way downstairs to rendezvous with the couch, the newspaper, and a bowl of chocolate chip ice cream.

I had barely spooned the ice cream into my bowl when I heard little footsteps in the hall.

"Daddy," Elizabeth said, "Jon keeps turning the light on."

I strode purposefully to the foot of the stairs. "Jonathan!" I bellowed, my voice firm and slightly menacing. "You turn that light off and leave it off!"

"Okay, Daddy," he said softly.

That, I was sure, was that. I returned to the kitchen and had just enough time to put the ice cream back in the freezer before I heard those footsteps again.

"Daddy," Elizabeth said, "Jon's bugging me."

This time I ran halfway up the stairs. "Jonathan, you leave your sister alone!" I roared. "If I have to come up here one more time, there's going to be serious trouble for one little boy!"

"Okay, Daddy," Jon said softly.

I returned to my ice cream, settled on the couch, and started scanning the headlines. This time, I didn't hear the footsteps. "Daddy," Elizabeth said, "Jon is singing, and he won't stop!"

That's it, I thought as I stormed upstairs. I've tried to be patient, but now it's time to . . .

I burst into his room. Jonathan sat up in bed and looked at me fearfully, uncertain.

"Jonathan!" I said angrily. "What are you doing?"

Tears began to form in his eyes. "Thinging," he said (in those days, Jon struggled with the letter s). Then he started to . . . well . . . thing: "Eenthie-weenthie 'pider went up the water 'pout . . ." He stopped. Then, in a hopeful voice, he asked, "Will you thing with me?"

My anger melted as I looked into his alert, glistening, and definitely unsleepy eyes. I was the one who had decided to put him to bed so early. Who could blame him for being a little antsy? So we "thang" a few quiet songs. We gave each other more hugs and kisses. I re-tucked him in, only this time it was gentle and unhur-ried. When he said his last "good night," his voice was calm and—believe it or not—tired.

And that was the last we heard from him—or Elizabeth—that night.

Maybe the whole process just wore him out. Or maybe I'm the world's worst singer. Still, I'm inclined to believe that we can accomplish more with our children through sweetness, gentleness, and patience than we can with anger and harsh threats. Of course, discipline is an important concept for our children to learn, and parents do them a disservice if they don't hold their kids' feet to the fire of consequence once in a while. But I can't help but think that the writer of Proverbs was thinking of parents when he wrote that "a soft answer turneth away wrath: but grievous words stir up anger."

Even at the end of a long, tiring day.

Especially at the end of a long, tiring day.

Rediscovered Hero

I don't look a thing like my father.

In his prime he had a full head of gloriously red hair; mine is sort of a mousey, dishwater blond-brown-blah. He has bright, penetrating blue eyes; mine are a noncommittal hazel (no matter how big your box of crayons is you won't find a crayon called "hazel"—trust me). He has a proud, prominent, almost Romanesque nose; mine is a squishy little blob in the middle of my face. And even at 93 years of age he has broad shoulders, strong arms, and large, powerful hands; my shoulders are narrow, my arms are reed-like, and my hands are soft, almost feminine.

Not that there is anything wrong with feminine hands. They look great on women. But they don't look virile and masculine. Like my dad's.

Which is why I was startled when an older gentleman stopped me in the mall the other day. "Aren't you Bud Walker's son?" he asked.

"Yes, I am," I said. "I'm his youngest son, Joe."

"I thought so," the gentleman said. "He used to speak of you often."

Now, you need to know that it has been years since Dad has spoken to anyone about anything. Time and disability have robbed him of one of his greatest natural abilities: his ability to communicate. Dad had a way with words and a way with people that I always admired and wanted to emulate. These days Dad is in a care center, where his warm smile and pleasant disposition endear him to all.

But he isn't talking—about me or anything else.

So after bringing the gentleman in the mall up to date on my father's condition, I had to ask him how he could, after so many years, remember Dad—not to mention Dad's youngest son.

The man paused, then said simply: "Your father is one of my heroes."

I could understand that. Dad was my hero, too. But

somehow, in caring for him through his current difficulties, I had forgotten the bright, vibrant, charismatic man he once was.

Until I was reminded by a stranger.

"Years ago when I was starting out in the life insurance business your father took me under his wing," he explained. "He taught me how to sell, but more important, he taught me how to serve my clients and develop relationships of trust and understanding with them. I've tried to run my business that way ever since. I couldn't have done it any other way.

"But that isn't the real reason your dad is my hero," the man continued. "One time a group of us from the main office went to a convention in Las Vegas. I had never been on one of these trips, but I had heard stories, you know? And sure enough, that first night a group of the guys were making plans to go places and do things that . . . well, married men shouldn't do.

"I wanted to be one of the guys, but I didn't want to do this. So I asked: 'Is Bud going?' The other guys kind of looked at each other and laughed. One of them said,

'Bud's a great guy and everything, but he doesn't know how to relax and have a good time.'

"That's all I needed to hear. I just smiled at the guy and said, 'You know what? Neither do I.' I figured if your dad could have a career without compromising his values, so could I.

"I've had a good career," the man concluded, "and in two months my wife and I are going to celebrate our 50th wedding anniversary. Following your dad's example has been part of both."

I didn't find what I was looking for at the mall that day. But I found something even better: a rediscovered hero.

Even if I don't look a thing like him.

What's in a Name?

It had been a long, brutal day on the sales floor for young Brent. He'd had his share of "ups"—that's what retail sales people call it when it's their turn with the next customer—and more than his share of downs. And now he was in danger of being shut out for the day.

And he hadn't been shut out in a long time. Even in his early days with the company he could always sell something to someone. That's why they made him assistant manager so quickly. He was good. A natural. And he had a knack for turning new customers into repeat customers.

But on this day, there were no customers. At least, none who wanted to buy. There were plenty who wanted to look, and he'd spent a lot of time with each one of those. But he could never close the deal. This, of course, exposed him to some good-natured ribbing from his associates, who took a not-so-secret delight in seeing the sales prodigy get his comeuppance.

There was more at stake here than professional pride and reputation, however. Brent is a new father. He and his wife, Kay, decided that she would be a full-time mom, which meant he would support the family. When he does well on the sales floor, that isn't a problem. But when he struggles, the whole family struggles.

And on this day, at least, he was struggling.

Toward the end of the day, a man came in shopping for a new suit. It had the potential to be a good sale, the kind that can turn a bad day into a good one—just like that. Brent worked hard to make it happen. The man tried on several suits. Brent carefully described the fabrics, pointed out the craftsmanship, and explained why these suits, though expensive, were such a good buy.

The man hesitated. Brent knew all too well the look he saw in his eyes—the look of a potential customer about to walk out the door empty-handed—and he was tempted to use some of the tricks he had learned to pressure people into making a purchase. But he had long since decided that wasn't the way he wanted to do business. So when it became clear that the man was going to leave to do a little comparison shopping, Brent handed him his business card and invited him to return after he'd had a chance to look around.

The man looked at Brent's card, and then took a long look at Brent. "So you're Brent's boy," the man said, alluding to the fact that the card identified him as Brent Jr.

"Do you know my dad?" Brent asked.

"Sure do," the man said. They chatted for a moment, establishing the link between father and son. Then the man said: "Your dad's a good man. If you're anything like him . . . well, tell me again about that suit."

Brent made the sale. But that wasn't why he called his father that night to recount the story. "I just wanted to thank you," he said, "for giving me a name I can be proud of."

There were tears in Brent Sr.'s eyes as he hung up the phone and gratitude in his heart that for all of the dumb things he had done in his life—and we all do them, don't we?—he hadn't done anything dumb enough to dishonor the name he shared with his son.

Or to make a long, brutal day on the sales floor even longer. Or more brutal.

No Jerk Policy

All in all, it was shaping up to be a bad day as we traveled home after the family reunion.

For one thing, the sleeping accommodations at the hotel hadn't been all that pleasant. For another, we stopped for gas and paid $3.67 per gallon. $3.67! I didn't pay that much for my first car (Okay, so it was a beat-up old Buick that my father gave to me on the condition that I pay for the repairs myself—I think you get my point).

And for a third, as we were driving we came upon a horrifying accident that had traffic at a standstill for 10 or 12 miles. Even though the accident was southbound and we were northbound, it sort of had me wondering if it was an omen of highway uckiness to come—for us.

Then we pulled into our favorite restaurant for breakfast. If ever there was a way to lift our spirits, it was a waffle or some French toast or an omelet at this place. There was even a parking spot right up front despite a crowded parking lot. I thought things were looking up until I paused by the sidewalk to let Anita and the kids jump out of the car before I parked it. While they were sliding out the door, a gentleman in a sporty little car pulled around me and into the parking space I was signaling my intent to enter.

"Oh, man," I thought, fatalistically. "Here we go. More bad stuff on a bad day."

Not being the confrontational sort, I sighed, shifted my car into reverse, and prepared to back up and go in search of another parking spot. But as I glanced toward the sporty little car that had taken my spot, I noticed the man and the woman inside were talking. She was pointing at me, and he was looking in my direction. Then I saw his reverse lights come on as he backed out of the spot he had "stolen" from me. He rolled down his window as he approached me.

"I am so sorry," he said. "I didn't notice that you were signaling to move into that spot."

Well, this was something I wasn't expecting. And I wasn't exactly sure how to react.

"Hey, it's survival of the fastest out here," I said. "It's yours if you want it."

"Nah," he said. "I hate it when people steal my spot. I couldn't do that to someone else."

"And I wouldn't let him," his wife said, forcefully, from the passenger's seat.

They smiled and waved and drove back into the parking lot, leaving the space up front for me. I walked into the restaurant feeling uplifted and revitalized, with a new positive outlook toward what was surely going to be a good day. Orange juice never tasted sweeter, nor was there ever a finer, fluffier omelet than the one I enjoyed that morning. Even the English muffin I ordered came to me slightly burned around the edges—just the way I like it!

As we prepared to go I noticed the couple from the sporty little car finishing breakfast. I stopped to thank them again for their act of kindness, but they shrugged it off as no big deal.

"Life is too short," he said, "to waste any time or energy on being a jerk."

I know—I was stunned by his unique philosophy, too. We live in a time when people seem to be more concerned about protecting what they perceive to be their rights than they are in doing what is actually right, and we don't mind being a jerk about it if that's what it takes. I'm as guilty of it as anyone (an awkward encounter with a crotchety older woman at a recent ball game comes to mind). But I was so inspired by this couple's "no jerk" policy that I found myself trying to live by it for the rest of the trip home—as a motorist, as a customer, and as a husband and father—and you know what? It turned out to be a pretty darn good day for all of us.

So I commend the philosophy to you. Honestly, it isn't as hard as it sounds. When it comes right down to it, it's really pretty simple: don't be a jerk.

And have a good day.

Miracles of Forgiveness

"Joe? Is that you?"

The woman speaking to me at the baseball game looked vaguely familiar.

"Marci?"

"It IS you!" she exclaimed, smiling broadly. "Gosh, it's good to see you again!"

It was good to see Marci, too. Off and on during the past few decades I've wondered about her. I almost tried to track her down a few years ago after talking to a mutual friend who had indicated that the 1980s had been pretty rocky for Marci. So bumping into her at the baseball game was, at the very least, fortuitous.

We spent a few minutes catching up on the business of our lives: kids and careers, spouses and houses, education and recreation (it's always a little disconcerting to see how few words are required to summarize 25 years of living). We played a little "have you seen . . . ?" and "did you know . . . ?" and we reminisced about the good old, bad old days.

Then Marci grew quiet for a moment, looking out over the crowd milling about the concession area. "You know, Joe," she said, "I've always wanted to tell you . . . how . . . you know. . . . how sorry I am for the way I treated you."

I squirmed. One does not like to remember when one has been unceremoniously dumped.

"It's okay," I said. "No big deal." *At least,* I thought to myself, *not now.*

"But I was such a jerk," she continued.

Yes, you were, I thought. But what I said was, "We were both pretty young."

"I know," she said. "But that's no excuse for . . ." She hesitated, then continued. "It's just always bothered me, remembering how mean I was to you. And I've wanted to tell you that I'm sorry. So . . . I'm sorry."

The smile on her face was warm and sincere. And there was something in her eyes—it looked a lot like relief—that melted any vestiges of icy resentment that I may have been harboring over the years since she had played pepper with my heart.

"Okay," I said. "Apology accepted!" Overcome by the sweetness of the moment, I reached an arm around her and gave her a quick hug. Just then, the crowd erupted with a huge cheer, and Marci and I both returned our attention to the game. By the time I looked over to where she had been, she was gone. But the warm, wonderful feeling of our brief exchange was still there and continues to this day whenever I think about it.

We all carry unpleasant, discomforting memories of deeds done or left undone and words said or unsaid. And we all bear wounds—some slight, some not-so-slight— that have been inflicted upon us by others. The healing balm of forgiveness can soothe a troubled conscience and bring peace to an injured soul—even years after the fact.

Of course, it isn't enough to just say "I'm sorry" and "You're forgiven." Though there is indeed great power in those simple words, that power is not available to those who are insincere or who are only looking for a way to further control, manipulate, or exploit. But when those words are truly felt and sincerely expressed, they can open the door to miracles of the heart and soul— miracles of forgiveness.

Even at a baseball game.

Stand Up for the Fourth

Dad was, by nature, a "stand up" guy.

Whenever a card game got intense, he'd stand up to make his play. Whenever he watched me play basketball or football he never sat in the stands with the other parents; he always stood by the side of the bleachers—usually alone. Whenever I came home late from a date, I'd sit on the couch and he'd stand in front of me to lecture—usually with a little pacing thrown in for good measure. And I don't remember ever seeing him sit down during a long telephone conversation. Anything over five minutes, he'd stand up.

That's just the kind of a guy he was. Forthright. Direct. You know—stand up.

One Fourth of July we were on the front row for our town's annual Independence Day Parade. Dad had gone down to Main Street early to set our folding chairs along the curb, so we had a great spot from which to watch the floats and bands and beauty queens pass by. We had just settled into our seats when a snare drum cadence signaled the start of the parade.

Looking to our right we could see four men in ill-fitting World War II uniforms marching down the middle of Main Street, carrying the red, white, and blue of the United States of America. Their eyes were fixed forward and they marched with clear direction and purpose, apparently unaware that their tummies were hanging ponderously over their government-issue belts.

But we were aware. To tell the truth, it was hard to miss. Some of the folks around me were chuckling and chatting about the veterans, who were so clearly past their prime. A couple of teenagers in the back shouted out jeers and taunts—this was, after all, the Vietnam War era, and such disrespect for the flag and for those who fought under it was common. Patriotism was unpopular, and in some settings even risky.

I don't know exactly when my father stood up and took his hat from his head and placed it over his heart.

He did it quietly, almost unobtrusively—I didn't even see him do it. But Dad wasn't a small man, and it didn't take long for the rowdies in the back to notice.

"Down in front!" one of them shouted.

"Yeah," another chimed in. "Down in front!"

Suddenly I realized they were yelling at my father, who continued to stand at attention, his eyes riveted on the stars and stripes. Nervously, I looked at Dad, willing him with all my heart and soul to sit down and not draw any more attention to himself—and to me, who wouldn't stand a chance against any of those high school boys. Then I looked at the feisty boys in the back, who were clearly not pleased that my father was blocking their view.

"Hey, Mr. Hawk," came another shout. "Find a place to perch!"

I had no idea why they called Dad "Mr. Hawk." I didn't know anything about the hawk-dove designations that were being used all around the country to character-ize pro-war and anti-war sentiments. I just knew my father's propensity for standing was attracting some undesirable attention, and I was feeling embarrassed—and a little threatened.

But then an interesting thing happened. Another man about Dad's age stood up a few feet away. He looked at the boys, then turned and faced the flag and put his hand over his heart. Then a woman to Dad's right did the same thing, and she tugged her husband to stand up with her. Then another couple, then an elderly woman, then an entire family right in front of the rowdies. Before the color guard had passed, the entire section of parade-goers—with the exception of a few high school boys— was standing at attention with their hands over their hearts.

Not a word was spoken by those who stood up for the flag. But a message was sent loud and clear to those teenagers—and to me. Patriotism isn't just something you feel. Sometimes, it's something you DO.

Whether or not you are, by nature, a stand up guy.

Making Ethel Smile

Her name was Ethel. I didn't know it at the time, of course. To tell the truth, it really didn't matter. All that mattered was that the music was playing, the dance floor was beckoning, she was woman, I was man. Let's dance.

I know, I know—I'm married. It's all right. My wife, Anita, was on the same dance floor, cutting a rug with a good-lookin' guy named Clarence. That's sort of the way it is during dances at the nursing home. You come, you see who is ambulatory, you dance.

We had gone to the nursing home "hoedown" to be with Dad, who is a resident there. But my sister, my daughters, and my wife were handling Dad's dancing needs, which left me free to check out the female talent. I danced with several women, including one who whistled—loudly and beautifully—throughout the song and with another who began screaming when I asked her name. They were all wonderful ladies, and I enjoyed each moment of musical movement—even when that "movement" consisted mainly of keeping my partner from falling down (sort of reminded me of a sorority dance I was invited to in my college days—but I digress).

Ethel, however, was special. There was fire in her eyes and passion in her voice. When I asked if she would like to dance, she responded brightly: "Yes, I would!" Her eyes never left mine as we danced. When I asked her name, she said, "My name is Ethel!" When I asked if she liked dancing, she told me, "Yes, I do!" When I told her she was a good dancer, she replied, "Yes, I am!" Always brightly. Always with energy. Always with grace.

But never with a smile. For some reason, during all of our pleasant interaction, she never smiled at me. Not once. After our dance was over and I had returned her to her seat, I asked one of the care center employees if there was a reason why Ethel couldn't smile.

"No," I was told. "She can smile. She just doesn't smile very often."

Well, that sounded like a challenge to me. So I spent

the rest of the evening trying to make Ethel smile. I told her both of my jokes (note to self: a care center for Alzheimer's patients probably isn't the best place to try out a comedy routine). I brought her food. I made faces at her while I was dancing with other women. She watched me carefully—almost intensely. She nodded at the jokes, thanked me for the food, and made faces back at me. But she didn't smile.

I was about to go Jerry Lewis on her—you know, drop my pants, fall on the floor, break a vase over my head, or try some other sophisticated form of comedy— when something funny happened. Or didn't happen, as the case may be. Clarence, Anita's former dance partner, wandered over to Ethel and sat next to her. He reached over and gently patted her hand. She looked at him. He smiled at her. She smiled back. Simple as that. The smile I had been working for all night was given to Clarence for just a pat and a grin. It wasn't fair. Unless . . .

"They're married, aren't they?" I asked the attendant. "Or maybe sweethearts?"

"Nah," she said. "They're just friends."

I've heard that phrase before—"just friends"—and

I'm not exactly sure what it means. It seems to infer a relationship that somehow lacks something. But my experience has been that a good and trusted friend is more than just . . . well . . . "just." Friendship is an extraordinary thing. It can bring depth to your life, comfort to your soul, joy to your heart, and a smile to your face.

Just ask Ethel.

Explaining the Inexplicable

It's a calm, bright, sunny day today. The kind of day that gives summer its glowing reputation. The kind of day for which the word *lolling* was invented. The kind of day that was just made for a tumbler of ice cold lemonade, a hammock stretched between billowing shade trees, and a radio play-by-play of today's game from Wrigley Field.

Ah, yes—summer. Hot dogs. Swimmin' holes. Blue skies. Fresh-cut grass. Lazy, hazy, crazy days spent peaceably. Serenely. Comfortably. Calmly.

Summer.

I mention this because yesterday was a different kind of summer day. It started out . . . well, summerishly. But by noon, dark threatening storm clouds had gathered to blot out the sun. The morning's gentle summer breeze turned into a gale-force wind, then into something even more sinister and frightening. The thick finger of a funnel emerged from the clouds, swirling its way toward the earth. Within moments a tornado was blasting through the downtown area not five miles from where I was working, cutting a wide swath of destruction, injury, and even death.

Local meteorologists are still trying to explain how a tornado could have touched down in our tranquil valley. The mountains that surround us are supposed to protect us from such things. At least, that's what my seventh-grade science teacher said. And that's what a friend of mine told her 5-year-old recently after the little girl saw *The Wizard of Oz* for the first time.

"Don't worry, sweetheart," my friend said when her daughter crawled into bed with her after a twister-related nightmare. "We don't get tornadoes here. The mountains protect us."

Moments after the tornado touched down, my friend dashed for the phone to call her daughter at home. Like

Ricky Ricardo and local meteorologists, she had some serious "splainin'" to do.

Well, nobody asked me—they never do; they know better—but I have an explanation. It is that sometimes there is no explanation. Sometimes during our precarious journey through life, stuff just happens—stuff that defies description or explanation. Natural disasters occur. Random acts of violence resulting in the loss of innocent life are acted out. Even good things happen—things for which there is no discernable rhyme or reason. They just happen. That's the nature of our existence on this planet. And for a big chunk of the time we spend here, no mortal explanation is possible—or even necessary.

Of course, that doesn't stop us from trying to explain the inexplicable. Every time one of these phenomena occur—natural or manmade—we trot out "experts" who theorize and hypothesize and otherwise-ize. During the last 24 hours, I've heard a lot of that relative to our tornado. But if you listen carefully and peer closely between the lines, you'll see that what they're saying is, essentially, "Hey, sometimes stuff happens"—only they're saying it in a really educated, erudite way.

And that's okay. Thankfully, our success in life isn't determined by our answers to "why" questions. When it comes right down to it, success and peace and happiness have less to do with external forces acting upon us than with how we choose to react to those forces. It's a matter of attitudes, not platitudes. Because the fact is, none of us can control what happens to us. We can't bottle sunshine or lasso the wind. But we can control our responses to the stuff that happens. And if we can control our responses and reactions, then it doesn't really matter what happens.

Or why.

Chicken Salad for the Procrastinator's Soul

There wasn't anything wrong with the chicken salad. It was quite tasty, actually. I especially liked the little pieces of cashew in the mixture—but then, I'm sort of nuts about nuts.

Elizabeth, however, is not. In fact, our then-10-year-old daughter is allergic to peanuts. Horribly so. If she touches a peanut product—or someone who has touched a peanut product—she breaks into a rash. And if she eats anything with peanuts or peanut butter in it . . . well, it can get ugly. Fast.

That's why she reacted to the chicken salad that was served at a recent reception. It was those bits of cashew (cooked in peanut oil, it turns out) that got to her. Within minutes, her eyes were red, her throat was scratchy, and her whole head was congested—clear indications of an allergic reaction.

So what did I do? Well, I did what I thought any good father would do under the circumstances. I told her to tough it out. Then I munched down another chicken salad sandwich.

"But, Dad, I really don't feel good," she said, huge tears welling up in her eyes.

"I know, honey," I said. "But there can't be much peanut oil on one little piece of cashew. Drink some water. Eat a mint. Sit and rest. It'll pass and you'll be fine."

Elizabeth looked appealingly to her mother, who suggested it wouldn't be such a bad idea to take our daughter home. "All right," I said. "But, Elizabeth, I want you to put on your pajamas and get ready for bed. No TV. No playing. If you're too sick to stay, you're too sick to play."

I know—I should have been a poet. What can I say? Chicken salad is my muse.

Elizabeth didn't protest, which should have been my first clue that this wasn't a glorified bout of hay fever or a ruse to get out of the reception. Still, I was startled when her little brother bounded down the stairs in a panic.

"Elizabeth can't breathe!"

Thankfully, that was a slight overstatement. She was breathing, but she was struggling to do so. She could barely force out enough air to speak, she was trembling like a leaf, and her lips were beginning to turn a frightening shade of blue. We had her out the door, into the car, and on the way to the hospital before I could even think of a rhyme for "Your father is an idiot."

Interestingly, none of the skilled professionals working in the emergency room that night told Elizabeth to tough it out or to drink some water or to eat a mint. They heard the words "allergic reaction" and sprang into action with death-defying speed and dexterity. She received a shot of Adrenalin, a steroid IV, and an oxygen mask within minutes of her arrival in the E.R., and before long my daughter was resting comfortably—with wonderfully pink lips.

Two hours later we were on our way home, but not before the doctor delivered a short-but-stern lecture. "You almost waited too long," he said. "As soon as she reacts, you react."

His words were chilling, and have stayed with me from that moment to this: "You almost waited too long." What did he mean by that? What might have happened had we waited longer? I don't even like to think about it. How could I ever forgive myself for waiting too long?

And how many times have I done that in my life—you know, waited too long? Have I waited too long to praise, to give a word of encouragement, to console, to comfort, to say "I'm sorry"? I'm sure I have. But no more. From now on I'm going to react more quickly to the needs of those around me, to do what needs to be done when it needs to be done—just like the doctor said. His words were like Adrenalin for my hesitant heart, or chicken soup for this procrastinator's soul.

Uh, better make that chicken salad. And hold the cashews.

The Privilege and Blessing of Work

It has always struck me as more than just a little bit ironic that every fall America pays tribute to her working men and women by not working.

Not that I'm complaining. I appreciate a day off as much as the next worker bee. It's just the logic that throws me. I mean, on Thanksgiving we actually give thanks. On Christmas we celebrate a gift from God by giving gifts ourselves. On Easter we observe another divine gift by eating multi-colored eggs that were supposedly delivered by a rabbit.

Okay, so the logic of Easter eludes me, too.

Still, it stands to reason that if we are going to celebrate America's workers, there ought to be something laborious about it. And no, I'm not talking about the effort it requires to pack a picnic lunch or to go camping or boating or any of the pastimes we work so hard at enjoying during the long weekend. I'm talking about sweating. Toiling. Working. You know—laboring.

Mom and Dad understood the concept. Around our house, Labor Day was just that: a day to labor. I don't remember any Labor Day picnics or parties or barbecues. We'd just had a full summer for that. Labor Day meant that school was back in session, and it was time to work.

And so we did. We prepared the garden bed for winter. We pruned fruit trees. We bottled peaches and pears and tomatoes until the inside of our house was thick with steam and aroma. Sometimes there were special projects that we hadn't finished during the summer: painting the trim around the house; taking out an old, dead stump; planting new grass in that patch of dirt in the middle of the lawn that we used as home plate during spirited games of Whiffle ball.

For me, however, the job was always the same: mowing, edging, and raking the lawn. As the youngest of eight children, I always got the easiest—and most boring—

duty. "It's not fair!" I protested one Labor Day. "I do the lawn all summer. Why can't somebody else do it today?"

"Because everyone else already has a job," Mom said.

So much for labor negotiations.

A late summer trip had interrupted regularly scheduled lawn care that year, and our yard looked it. The grass was tall and thick—especially the edges. I shuddered. Dad didn't believe in power mowers or edgers, so this would require hours of back-breaking, wrist-snapping, energy-sapping labor.

What a way to spend Labor Day, huh?

Don't ask me how, but I survived the ordeal. I was tired from pushing the mower up and down the slope of our front lawn. My fingers ached from squeezing Dad's rusty grass clippers. And I was itchy from the grass that seemed to cover me. But for some reason, as I sat out on the front porch looking out over the aesthetic results of my labors, none of that mattered. I was weary, but content. And I wasn't sure why until Mom came out with the lemonade.

"That's why we have you mow the lawn," she said as she handed me a tall, cool glass. "You do such a good job."

In retrospect, I'm sure other lawns in our neighborhood looked as good as ours. Maybe better. But that night I was King Lawnboy, and all was right in my carefully clipped kingdom.

I've never forgotten the feeling of satisfaction that came from a job well done. That's the feeling we ought to celebrate on Labor Day, for much of what we are as a nation we owe to the efforts of workers who are willing to work and who take pride in the results of their labors. So do something laborious this Labor Day, and savor the privilege and blessing of work.

'Tis the season, you know.

Sorry, Forgiven . . . and Accountable

Joe made a mistake—a big one. He knew it. And now, everyone was going to know about it—thanks to the police.

"Excuse me, sir," said the officer who came to our door, "but do you know a little boy with blond hair, six years old or so, who is wearing blue shorts and a blue and red striped shirt?"

I glanced at blond-haired Joe, who was six years old at the time and who was wearing blue shorts and a blue and red striped shirt as he sat watching *He-Man* on TV. He took one look at the policeman and burst into tears.

"I didn't mean to do it!" he said. "Don't let them take me to jail!"

Obviously, something had happened that I needed to

know about. I turned to the officer for an explanation. "He was throwing rocks at cars," he said. "He hit one. Did some damage."

I looked at Joe. His chin quivered. He looked at me with tear-filled eyes and nodded. I didn't know whether to hug him or spank him. So I turned to the officer: "What should we do?"

"Under the circumstances, the owner of the car isn't inclined to press charges," he said. "But he would appreciate an apology, and he thinks you ought to help him get his car fixed."

That was only fair, I agreed. The policeman gave me the car owner's address, and after a lecture to Joe about not throwing rocks at cars, the officer left. I picked up the lecture where the policeman left off. Now, it should be noted that I am a notorious lecturer. My lectures are so long, my children don't measure them in terms of minutes, they measure them in terms of shoe sizes ("My feet grew two sizes during that lecture.") And I am prone to flights of fancy that defy description—and logic. I have been known to cover Egyptian architecture, the life span of various marsupials, Wilt Chamberlain's impact on basketball, and the wit and wisdom of the Monkees during a lecture on taking out the trash.

So we had pretty much covered the dangers of rock-throwing and respect for the property of others—not to mention Peruvian horticulture and the sociological implications of Gilligan's Island—by the time we got to the car owner's house. I was hoping to see a beat-up truck in the driveway. Unfortunately, it was a beautiful red Camaro, with a glaring scratch and dent on one door.

"Do we have to do this?" Joe asked as we stood at the car owner's door.

"Yep," I said.

See? I can be brief.

"But what should I say?"

"Tell him you're sorry."

Which is just what Joe did. His apology was short, nervous, and sincere. The car owner told Joe that he forgave him, that he understood that kids make mistakes, but that it was really important not to throw rocks at cars. Then he talked to me about getting his car fixed.

It was that last part that Joe didn't understand. "If he

forgives me," he asked as we made our way home, "why do we still have to pay for it?"

"Because his car is still damaged, and the damage is still our fault," I explained. "Your saying 'I'm sorry' and him saying 'I forgive you' doesn't change that."

I'm not sure Joe understood completely. It's a difficult concept to grasp, even for those who are older and more experienced. Some of us forget that forgiveness and accountability are not mutually exclusive and that being sorry—and being forgiven—doesn't free us from the consequences of the choices we make. We can be sorry, forgiven, and accountable.

Even if our mistake is big, and everyone knows about it.

Miracles of Faith, Trust, and Hope

Set aside your skepticism. Cast away doubt. Miracles do happen.

And I'm feeling sort of guilty about it.

The miracle in this case is Carley Jo, a 4-year-old with a badly diseased heart. Her doctors had hoped to delay heart surgery until she was older and much, much bigger—about 40 pounds or so heavier. And she seemed to be doing well; watching her chatter and play—both non-stop—it was difficult to think of her as dangerously ill. It was only when she would occasionally come in from playing, pale and trembling, to tell her mommy that her heart hurt that you realized what a precarious life-and-death struggle was being waged within that tiny chest.

About four weeks ago her doctors announced that

the surgery could be delayed no longer. As difficult as it would be to perform open heart surgery on a 35-pound child, they simply had to proceed—immediately. At first the doctors appeared to be pretty positive about Carley Jo's prognosis. As the day of the operation approached, however, the chances of success dipped to about 50–50. Then the day before the surgery, Carley Jo's parents met with the surgeon who would perform the operation. The esteemed physician, a man of considerable skill and significant reputation, sat with his head in his hands, rubbing his temples, as he talked about how difficult the operation was going to be, and how he wasn't sure he could do it.

Not exactly encouraging, if you know what I mean.

"Look, if you're not sure you can do this, or that it's even going to work, why are we doing it?" Carley Jo's mommy, Michelle, wanted to know.

"Because I'm certain of what will happen if we don't do the surgery," the doctor replied.

He didn't need to explain. Michelle and her husband, Brian, were painfully aware of the consequences of that option, which really wasn't an option at all. Of course they would ask the doctors to perform the surgery. And they would ask God to perform a miracle.

Which is exactly what He did. To say that the operation was a success is a little like saying Tiger Woods is a successful golfer. Not only did they do the needed repairs, but they were also able to take care of another problem that would have required future surgery. The surgeon—the same guy who wasn't sure he could do it— said he couldn't have done it better.

And no, he wasn't being boastful. He was in awe.

"That wasn't my best work in there," he told Brian and Michelle after the operation. "That was better than my best. I can't really explain it other than to say I had help."

Carley Jo agreed. The day after her operation, she told her father that there were angels in the operating room. "Did you see them?" Brian asked.

"No," Carley Jo replied. "But I know they were there."

Nobody familiar with the situation doubts it. And we're grateful—to the surgeon, to the angels, to God. But I can't help but look around and see other children who don't fare so well. Children whose surgeries are less successful. Children who never make it to surgery. Children who suffer abuse of all kinds. Children who desperately need an angel—until they become one. Where is their miracle? And why did our miracle come through when theirs did not?

If you're expecting to find answers to those questions here . . . well, that would take another miracle. All I can offer is faith, trust, and hope. Faith that God loves all of His children. Trust that He knows what is best for each of them. And hope that He never runs out of miracles.

Better the Devil, You Know

The chicken fajitas were cooking nicely—no question about it.

The tantalizing smells wafting from the Dutch oven simmering on the back patio were enough to tell you that. Chicken chunks, onions, peppers, tomatoes, and spices were mingling deliciously, and soon the steaming, aromatic mixture would be spooned onto warm tortillas and consumed by members of two appreciatively hungry families.

Unfortunately, that moment of triumphant consumption was still a few minutes away. Which wasn't a big problem for most of us, who could actually enjoy the last moments of anxious anticipation (and who, the truth be known, could actually stand to miss a meal now and then). But for 10-year-old Lexi, it was an issue. Lexi is diabetic and has to keep a close eye on her blood sugar levels. And the long wait for fajitas was pushing those levels to a point of mild concern.

What can I say? You just can't rush a Dutch oven.

So Lexi calmly got out her little insulin kit and prepared a syringe for one of her thrice daily injections. Based on her sugar level, she consulted with her mother in getting just the right dosage, then sat without flinching while her mother administered the shot.

Eleven-year-old Elizabeth, who regularly uses an inhaler in her daily battle with asthma, watched the process carefully. No stranger to the travails of ongoing medication, she seemed fascinated by what she saw Lexi doing. And as I tucked her into bed that night, it became quickly evident that what she had seen had touched her.

"Did you say your prayers?" I asked.

"Yes," she said. "I thanked God for my asthma."

As near as I could tell, that was a first. I couldn't remember ever hearing Elizabeth list "asthma" among her blessings. And so I gently asked why.

"It isn't that I like asthma," she said, simply. "But at least I don't have to take shots."

I understood immediately how she felt. Earlier in the week I had spoken to a friend who told me that her aged father had, within a few weeks' time, met and married a woman forty-two years his junior.

Oh, and did I mention that this "bride" has a criminal "rap sheet" longer than Shaquille O'Neal's arm? And that she has a long, sad history of drug abuse? And that she is HIV positive?

As you might expect, my friend is concerned. I tried to express support and my sincere hope that everything will turn out well for everyone involved, but I couldn't help but think of my own 90-year-old father, content and safe and well-cared for in a nearby care center. Maybe there are some things worse than having Alzheimer's. And I silently thanked God for my challenges, just as Elizabeth thanked God for her asthma.

Mom used to have a saying that expressed that sentiment: "Better the devil, you know." Of course, I didn't really understand that when I was growing up. I'd look around, and all I could see was how much better or easier or more exciting other people's lives seemed to be. But as I've grown older, I've come to understand that everyone has their share of struggles—visible or otherwise. And no matter how taxing my particular share of struggles may be, when I see what other people are going through with the challenges they are facing . . . well, I'll take mine.

Along with another helping of chicken fajitas, if you please.

Now You Know

It was lust at first sight. Or at the very least, gluttony.

I should have seen it coming. I've always had this thing for Chinese food. I consider ham fried rice to be one of the basic food groups, all by itself. I've been known to drive hours out of my way for good Mongolian barbecue. And the way I see it, if there's no sweet-and-sour in heaven, I'm not going.

So the first time I drove by the big Chinese buffet that is located just a few blocks west of the Alzheimer's care center where my dad resides, I knew I was in trouble.

"Look, Honey!" I said to my wife, Anita, as we drove past the building on our way to see Dad. "All-you-can-eat Chinese food!"

"Uh-huh," said Anita.

"Doesn't that sound wonderful?" I said, with visions of hot, steaming egg rolls dancing in my head. "And look—the parking lot is crowded. That's a good sign, isn't it?"

"Uh-huh. Joe, please keep your eyes on the road. You almost hit that Honda."

Obviously, Anita didn't understand that hitting a Honda was a small price to pay for really good stir-fry. Still, she humored me nearly every time we drove past the place, as I felt compelled to comment on how many cars were always in the parking lot and how science had proven a direct correlation between culinary excellence and automotive abundance.

Yes, I know. What can I say? It was the MSG talking.

Then last week it happened. After more than a year of driving past the Chinese buffet, the right combination of time and circumstances (in other words, I finally had a few dollars left in the checking account the day before payday) presented us with the opportunity to go in. Of course, we had to stand in line for a few minutes, which just added to the anticipation. And when we finally got inside and saw all of that Chinese food piled up and waiting for us, I thought I had died and gone to . . . well, whatever is the Chinese equivalent of Nirvana.

I skipped over the salad bar and went right to the good stuff: Egg foo yung. Fried rice. Sweet-and-sour chicken. Lo mein. Beef stir-fry. Mongolian barbecue. It all looked so good. It all smelled so good.

And it all tasted so bad.

Well, maybe "bad" is too harsh. But it wasn't good. It was just . . . bland. Tasteless. Uninspiring. And very disappointing. Anita, who had gone the salad bar route, could sense what I was feeling. It wasn't just a disappointing meal. It was a disappointing meal that I had been anxiously anticipating for more than a year.

"Well," she said, patting my hand reassuringly, "at least now you know."

And there's something to be said for that, I guess. Life doles out its share of disappointments, large and small, to all of us. Games are lost. Tests are failed. Relationships turn sour. Dreams turn into nightmares. Sometimes it's hard to find peace in failure. At such times, there is some consolation in simply knowing that . . . well, now you know. And you can deal with it and move on.

Come to think of it, I didn't even glance at that Chinese buffet when I drove by yesterday. And I didn't even come close to hitting a Honda.

Holding Hands with Elizabeth

Years from now when I think about the movie *Cast Away* I will remember a compelling storyline, some extraordinary special effects, and a remarkable acting performance by Tom Hanks.

But mostly I'll remember holding hands with Elizabeth.

We went to see the film as a family, which is why I wasn't sitting by my wife, Anita. We have found that keeping 11-year-old Elizabeth and her 9-year-old brother, Jon, away from each other is the best way to keep them from killing each other in the dark. It isn't that they fight all the time; it's just that we never know when a fight is going to erupt. So we sit between them, and hope they never figure out how to launch Milk Duds at each other over the top of us.

Just a few minutes into the movie—and I hope I'm not spoiling this for anyone—there's a frighteningly realistic plane crash. In fact, it was a little too frightening and a little too realistic for Elizabeth's taste. She leaned up against me, her head pressed against my shoulder, and reached over and took my hand, squeezing it tightly.

"It's okay, Sweetie," I said. "Remember, it's only a movie. Just close your eyes, and pretty soon it'll all be over."

And pretty soon it was. Within a few minutes the scary part was over for Elizabeth, and she was sitting up in her seat, happily independent, her hands busy with popcorn and soda.

It wasn't long, however, before another scary part came along. Only this wasn't a scary part for Elizabeth— this was a scary part for me. For as long as I can remember, I've been claustrophobic. You want to scare me to death? Put me in a crowded elevator—and then make it stop. So when Tom Hanks started exploring that cave, I started cowering in my seat. Heart pounding. Palms sweating. Afraid to look—afraid not to. And I'm thinking, *If there are any spiders or snakes in this cave, I'm outta here.*

Suddenly I felt a hand reaching out in the darkness—a calm, steady, 11-year-old hand, slightly seasoned with salt and butter-flavored topping. It grabbed onto my hand firmly, squeezing reassuringly, as Elizabeth again leaned up against me, her head again pressed against my shoulder.

"It's okay, Daddy," she said. "Remember, it's only a movie. Just close your eyes, and pretty soon it'll all be over."

And pretty soon it was. Only this time, I didn't let go of Elizabeth's hand after the scary part was over, and she didn't let go of mine. We just sat there through the rest of the movie, holding onto each other and helping each other through the film's subsequent ups and downs.

That's how Elizabeth and I made it through *Cast Away.* And it occurs to me that that's how we all make it through life, too. Although we like to think of ourselves as happily independent and self-reliant, when the scary parts of life come—as they always do, eventually—it's comforting to be able to lean against family and friends, to hear their reassurance that it's okay, and to reach out in the darkness to find a calm, reassuring hand.

With or without the butter-flavored topping.

Prayer Is the Answer

It was a simple, innocent question from someone I've never actually met.

"You probably pray," my young e-mail correspondent wrote. "If you don't mind me asking, what do you pray about? And why?"

I didn't mind. Although prayer is a deeply personal practice for people of all religious persuasions, I'm happy to talk about it. So I clicked on "reply" and prepared to be profound.

"You're right," I wrote, "I do pray. Faithfully."

Good start, I thought. I especially liked the double-meaning of "faithfully." I hoped my young e-friend would appreciate it.

"And when I pray," I continued, "I pray about . . ."

My mind started swimming. What DO I pray

about? And what can I say about prayer that would have meaning to someone who wasn't familiar with the role prayer can play in someone's life?

"I pray about . . . well . . . everything."

Duh! That doesn't tell her anything. Come on, Mr. Writer. Mr. Communicator. Mr. Holier-Than-None. Come up with the words that will help her understand what prayer has meant to you through forty-five years of living in-and-out of intimacy with God (and you'll have to tell her the truth—there has been more out than in).

Tell her about the times you prayed and felt like your words were racing on Heaven's Autobahn right straight to God—a feeling so exhilarating that it helped you through the other times, when you felt as though your words were bouncing off the ceiling and crashing to the floor around you. Tell her about the time your eldest sister felt impressed to pray for your eldest brother at precisely the same moment he was contemplating suicide 500 miles away, and how he was immediately filled with such a powerful feeling of peace that it turned his life around. Of course, you'll also have to tell her about the times you've prayed with all your heart and soul for stuff that . . . well, let's just say that you're still waiting for those answers.

Still, I pray. But why?

I pray because my parents prayed, and I saw how it imbued their lives with meaning.

I pray because I like how I feel when I pray: peaceful, hopeful, and optimistic.

I pray because I have two children at home, learning and growing in a world that sometimes isn't child-friendly.

I pray because I have a daughter in college, facing life on her own for the first time.

I pray because I have two newlywed children, trying to figure out marriage at a time when so many around them have quit trying.

I pray because I have a granddaughter.

I pray because I want to do everything I possibly can—everything—to support our military men and women, our law enforcement officers, our firefighters, and our ballot-counters.

I pray because . . . well, who else are you going to thank for that sunset?

I pray because I have a father with Alzheimer's.

I pray because I can never get through to Bill Gates.

I pray because I know how much fathers like to hear from their children.

I pray because I believe, and I believe because I pray.

And when it comes right down to it, that's the only answer that really counts.

When the Right Thing Turns Out Wrong

To tell you the truth, I don't remember all of the reasons why Ernesto came to live with us. As I recall, my brother, who was living in Chile at the time, told us Ernesto needed a place to stay in the United States. Inviting him to stay with us seemed like the right thing to do.

And for a while, things worked out really well. Ernesto was a gracious guest. It was fun teaching him American customs and helping him expand his English vocabulary and grammar. He had a pleasant personality, and his Latin good looks and charm were . . . well . . . charming.

Then the teasing began. At first, it was occasional, and playful. But gradually it became his way of communicating with my sister and me, and it became hurtful. Kathy was going through a gawky, insecure stage, and Ernesto was relentless in pointing out what he thought were personality and figure flaws. I, on the other hand, was a chunky child, and was painfully aware of how much larger I was than the other kids my age. I didn't know it at the time, but I had started into the first stages of bulimia. I would skip lunch at school because I was embarrassed to eat in front of people, and then I would take my lunch money to 7–11 to buy and eat as much junk food as I could get.

It wasn't much of a diet, especially since all of those empty calories only made me heavier. To their everlasting credit, my friends didn't say much about my weight, and even when a thoughtless comment slipped out I tended to laugh it off. But Ernesto wouldn't let it go.

"Hey, Gordo," he would say, replacing my name with the Spanish word for fat. "When are you going to start sleeping with the rest of the pigs?" Then he would grab the layer of fat around my middle and pinch—hard—until I started to cry, as much from the humiliation as from the pain.

"Pobrecito," he would say in mock sympathy. "Pobre bebé gordito."

My parents asked him to stop teasing us—several times, as I recall. But he didn't stop; he was just more careful about when he did it. Dad asked us to try to be forgiving.

"Maybe this is how people show affection in Chile," he reasoned. "We just need to be patient until he understands that hurting people isn't acceptable here."

But Ernesto saw our attempts at tolerance as weakness, which prompted him to press his advantage, threatening to make things even worse for us if we told Mom or Dad.

One night when I was taking a bath, Mom inadvertently walked in on me. For the first time she saw the purplish bruises on my sides. "How did you do that?" she asked.

"That's where Ernesto pinches me," I said.

By the time I got home from school the next day, Ernesto was gone, and I don't remember ever seeing him again. It was some time before I asked my dad about what happened.

"Well," he said carefully, "things just didn't work out."

"Yeah," I said. "I guess it wasn't such a good idea to have him come and live with us."

"No," Dad said, "it was a good idea. It was the right thing to do. It just didn't work out. Maybe it was his fault; maybe it was ours. Probably we all could have handled things better."

Then he taught me an important lesson: "Sometimes we do the right thing and it turns out wrong," he said. "Maybe somebody makes a mistake or handles something poorly, or maybe things just don't work out like we thought they should. That doesn't mean it was wrong. It just means that you tried to do what's right, and you did the best you could."

And that's the right thing to do—no matter how it turns out.

Sniffling Indefatigably

It was the sniffling, finally, that got to me.

Not the chin-ups on the light-rail train hand straps. Not the constant din of teenage cell phone chatter. Not even the almost overwhelming aroma of a diaper in desperate need of maintenance. None of these things bothered me about the family sitting across the aisle from me on the commuter train that afternoon.

Just the sniffling, emanating from a youngster I'd guess to be about ten years old.

It was constant.

Steady.

Indefatigable.

And if that wasn't a word (meaning "tireless" and "incessant") before I got on the train that day, it certainly was after. Because my little sniffling buddy was exactly that.

Tireless and incessant. You know—indefatigable.

And I wasn't the only one who noticed. The lady in the seat facing mine glanced up from her magazine more than once, glancing across the aisle at the raucous little family. She probably wondered as I did why the mother seemed to pay no attention to the aural explosions erupting from her son's sinuses. At one point the lady looked for all the world as though she was about to say something. But she hesitated, then buried her face in her magazine again.

It was just as well. What could she say in the face of something so . . . you know . . . indefatigable?

At the next stop, another woman boarded the train and sat down next to the lady reading the magazine. She was one of "those" commuters—you know the kind. Instead of avoiding eye contact, they look fellow passengers directly in the eye. Instead of earnestly avoiding human contact and interaction, they smile and chat amiably with anyone about anything. And instead of being overwhelmed by something indefatigable, they offer a tissue.

"Here you go, young man," she said, smiling. "Sounds like you could use this."

"Oh, thank you," the boy's mother said, relieved. "He's got allergies."

"Oh, I know," the new woman said. "I've got 'em too. And they've been awful this year."

"Tell me about it," the mother said. "I keep reminding him, don't go anywhere without some tissue. But he never listens."

"Well, if you think it's bad now, you just wait until he's a teenager," the new woman said. "Why, with my boys it was . . ." and she was off on a long story that extended for several stops and included references to teen drinking, body piercing, and Britney Spears.

Don't ask.

Meanwhile, I couldn't help but notice that the sniffling had stopped.

Completely.

Totally.

Blessedly.

Turns out indefatigability is no match for a stranger who cares.

And that's nothing to sneeze at.

Or sniffle, as the case may be.

God's Babies

Jon is the youngest of our five children. Our baby.

But at age ten, he doesn't SEEM like a baby.

He's just a few inches shorter than his mother—which isn't saying much, since Anita is sort of a shrimp. At the rate he's growing, he'll shoot past her in the next year or so, and before long he'll pass his sisters, and eventually his big brother and me as well. This is why Joe and I are trying to play as much basketball with him as we can now—while we still tower over him.

Jon is growing in other ways, too. He's doing great in school and somehow seems to have missed out on the infamous Walker Anti-Math gene. He gets along well with his friends and has even begun to notice that girls can be interesting—and fun. And when he accidentally learned about a certain Big Secret during the holiday season, he handled it with maturity and a level head—and only a few disappointed tears.

It's fun, watching him grow up—and kind of hard, too. He represents the end of an era for Anita and me, and to tell you the truth, it's an era I'm not altogether sure I'm ready to relinquish. I love being a dad. And yes, I know that I will always be "Dad" to my children, but somehow, it's not the same when your kids are old and on their own. For one thing, the older kids get, the more complicated—and expensive—their problems become. And for another, when they are old they don't see you as The Ultimate Source of All Truth and Knowledge—rather, you're just another pit stop on the information superhighway.

And usually the last pit stop, at that.

So when Jon got sick a couple of weeks ago, I was anxious to nurture and care for my child. And this illness gave me every opportunity to do so. We're still not exactly sure what the problem was, although we knew it wasn't serious. But whatever it was, it was a pain. Literally. Jon had gas pains in his stomach so intense, it doubled him over and brought tears to his eyes. And to mine.

The pains would come and go. Sometimes he would reach out for me.

"Daddy," he would cry, "it hurts!"

I would pick him up in my arms and carry him to the couch. He would lay there with his head in my lap, while I stroked his face and played with his hair. He seemed to like that.

And so did I.

Now, I'm not trying to say that I'm glad Jonathan got sick. It was hard to watch him suffer, hard to see the tears and the pain in his eyes. But I knew he was going to be okay, and I was glad I could be there to give him comfort and love and to help him through it.

As I sat there trying to soothe my son—hurting for him, and yet savoring the feeling of being there for him—I couldn't help but wonder if maybe sometimes God feels that way. He watches us. He sees us learning and growing, functioning independently, and feeling like we've got everything under control. Then something happens—something painful—and with tears running down our cheeks we reach out to Him.

"Oh, God," we cry, "it hurts!"

At such times, I can almost feel Him gathering us in His arms, His fingertips stroking our faces and playing with our hair—comforting us. Loving us. And helping us through it.

Not because He's God. But because He's our parent. And we're His babies.

Even if we don't SEEM like babies.

A Little Shot of Appreciation

On the surface, it appeared that Nicole had everything in the world going for her.

By any standard of measurement, she was a beautiful young woman. She had a bright, buoyant, bubbly personality that endeared her to teenagers and adults alike. She had lots of friends, and they were active in lots of different things. And she was deeply devoted to her faith.

When you saw Nicole you smiled, mostly because she was almost always smiling her happy, infectious smile. That's just the way she was, and she made others feel happy, too.

At least, that's how it appeared.

But deep inside, Nicole was crying. You see, she has

Attention Deficit Disorder (ADD), a neurological problem that is a learning disability. No matter how hard she tries to keep up in her classes, her mind just doesn't make many of the conceptual connections that other students make without even trying. She can understand what's being taught at any particular moment in time; she just can't put it together with other concepts to form a logical sequence of thoughts or events.

And that makes school pretty traumatic for her, and incredibly frustrating. She tries hard to keep up—or to at least cover her lack of understanding—but that just makes her anxious, stressed and, often, depressed. Self-esteem is the first casualty in a battle with ADD. Of course, only her family saw this side of her. She managed to keep up a happy, cheerful front among her friends at school, but her family saw the toll it was taking on her soul.

Her junior year of high school was especially challenging, and the whole family was suffering. They tried family counseling, and it helped a little. But as Nicole's senior year approached, the now-familiar feeling of pressure and dread began building, and the family geared up for one more agonizing year.

One night while Nicole was out with friends, Hannah, her 16-year-old sister, felt an overwhelming desire to communicate her feelings to Nicole. She took a notebook and sat on the front porch and began writing all the things she admired about her big sister and expressed her appreciation for the important role Nicole had played in her life. Love and heartfelt gratitude flowed onto the paper, and then Hannah folded it into an envelope and placed it on Nicole's pillow.

When Nicole came home, she had an attitude (parents of teenagers know exactly what I'm talking about). The night had not been particularly pleasant, and she just wanted to retreat to her room. She closed the door firmly behind her. Within moments her door burst open and she rushed to Hannah's room, tears streaming down her face and Hannah's letter clutched in her hand.

"You saw the prayer I wrote, didn't you?" Nicole said tearfully as she embraced her sister.

"No," Hannah replied through her own tears. "I didn't know you wrote a prayer."

Nicole showed her sister what she had written in her journal earlier that day: "Dear God, all I want is for somebody to appreciate me for who and what I am. That's all I want."

It's amazing what a little shot of sincere appreciation can do for someone lacking in the self-esteem department. Within a few weeks Nicole was standing in front of 600 peers at a youth retreat, publicly acknowledging her struggle with ADD, and expressing appreciation to Hannah—and to God. And while I won't say that her senior year was easy, she made it, and is now ready to move on with her life, looking once again like she has everything in the world going for her.

Whether or not she actually does.